SHRUBS
A GARDENER'S
HANDBOOK

SHRUBS
A GARDENER'S
HANDBOOK

IAN COOKE

THE CROWOOD PRESS

First published in 2012 by
The Crowood Press Ltd
Ramsbury, Marlborough
Wiltshire SN8 2HR

www.crowood.com

British Library Cataloguing-in-Publication Data
A catalogue record for this book is available from the British Library.

ISBN 978 1 84797 312 2

Frontispiece *Rhododendron yakushimanum* 'Sneezy'

Acknowledgements
Many thanks to all those who have helped with this book, filling gaps in my knowledge or supplying pictures. Thanks to the friendly garden owners who allowed me to dash over as soon as the sun shone and photograph shrubs in their gardens, during the rather dreary and unpredictable summer of 2010.

Particular thanks to Peter Moore, Jo Davey from John Wood Nurseries, Suzanne O'Neill from Bransford Webbs, Steven Lee from New Place Nurseries and Peter Bealtry from Genesis for information and pictures to illustrate the new plants section. Appreciation also to Fitzgerald Nurseries, John Wood Nurseries and my son Tom Cooke for pictures. Once again I thank Mike Coleman for patiently demonstrating propagation whilst I wielded the camera.

Credit finally to my partner Philip for his support and patience, and for supplying just the right word or phrase on various occasions when my brain failed to function.

Picture credits
All pictures are by the author with the exception of the following: p. 24, p. 74, p. 75 (upper), p. 90 Peter Moore; p. 25 Plant Heritage; p. 35, rear cover (lower right) Tom Cooke; p. 38, p. 55, p. 94, p. 97, p. 103, p. 109 Tony and Marie – Four Seasons Garden; p. 66 Melissa Scott; p. 72, p. 84 (upper), p. 87 (upper) Bransford Webbs; p. 73, p. 75 (lower), p. 81 (lower), p. 84 (lower), p. 86, p. 89 (lower) New Place Nurseries; p. 77 Fitzgerald Nurseries; p. 81 (upper) Genesis Plant Marketing; p. 91 (lower) John Wood Nurseries.

Typeset by Jean Cussons Typesetting, Diss, Norfolk
Printed and bound in India by Replika Press Pvt Ltd

CONTENTS

PREFACE

The very word shrubbery conjures up a picture for most of us of drab dripping laurels hanging over a weed-infested gravel driveway. Something from a Victorian novel, where the gardener is likely to appear furtively from behind a tree, pushing one of those ancient wheelbarrows with deep wooden sides and a squeaking steel wheel, crunching on mossy gravel! The picture may be curious but it's not attractive and neither is that sort of shrubbery.

My own childhood introduction to shrubs, although less gothic, was no more attractive. My parents lived in a corner plot and the front garden was enclosed by about eight enormous shrubs, probably growing to nearly 2.5m (8ft) each year. These were old-timers: ultra vigorous yellow *Forsythia*, red *Weigela*, *Deutzia* and white scented *Philadelphus*. Describing their flower colour is really a bit superfluous as they rarely blossomed. Each year it was my job to prune these monsters and under my father's instruction, each bush was cut to a regimental man-high hedgehog. Inevitably they didn't flower and the response the next year was another flush of vigorous growth, to my juvenile annoyance!

As a student at Writtle College, I soon discovered a whole world of wonderful shrubs with tantalizing flowers and fantastic foliage. Learning their names in the weekly plant identification test at a rate of twenty new plants each week was quite daunting, but I quickly realized that shrubs were the backbone of any good garden. Wanting to try these for myself I set about propagating them with a windowsill propagator, only to be chastised by the college authorities for stealing cuttings! I also at this time discovered the college's rubbish tip and retrieved for myself a whole range of discarded shrubs which became integral parts of the first garden I created. Theft and scavenging – what a career starter!

Over the years, I have had the opportunity to buy, grow and propagate thousands of shrubs. I used to joke in my last job that 'I gardened on a large scale at someone else's expense'. I have had the privilege of designing landscapes and buying shrubs and seeing them grow to maturity. A few have died, some have struggled to survive but by far the majority have grown and thrived, giving pleasure for many years. Shrubs are rewarding plants to grow.

To say that shrubs have it all might be an exaggeration. But amongst the huge range of shrubs that we can grow in our climate, there are species and cultivars that will do almost anything we might ask of them in the garden. You want scent, plant *Choisya ternata*. Need some coloured foliage, then *Elaeagnus;* winter flowers, try *Jasminum nudiflorum;* something tough to withstand salt spray, why not use tamarisk? Maybe not such a fraudulent claim!

Despite having worked with shrubs for over forty years, I have learnt much myself in researching this book, which has made it a pleasure to write. I hope others will find it enjoyable to read and share my enthusiasm for this huge group of fascinating plants.

OPPOSITE: **A traditional shrubbery in The Arboretum, Nottingham, a Victorian park complete with weedy gravel paths and dreary dripping evergreens.**

1 INTRODUCING SHRUBS

Together with trees, shrubs are probably the most important plants used in gardens and landscapes. Such woody plants form the permanent structure of any garden. They are sometimes spoken of as the skeleton of the landscape, which is then dressed with more ephemeral plants such as herbaceous perennials, ornamental grasses, bulbs and annuals. Good gardens and landscapes will probably include a range of all of these types of plants, but it is the woody plants that give the greatest impact. And although trees are vital in a garden for the height and the impact they give, it is the shrub components that probably make the greatest contribution to the overall landscape.

Shrubs are permanent and will, if properly maintained, grow for many years, contributing to the landscape throughout the year and getting better continually. Some will be evergreen and so make a greater contribution during the winter months. Even those that are deciduous and lose their leaves in the autumn still have a shape, and the tracery of their bare branches will have an effect during the winter months. During the winter months look at any garden that is based purely on herbaceous perennials and summer annuals and you will see how barren a garden can be without shrubs.

So what is a shrub?

Shrubs are woody plants with a permanent structure, with multiple branches and sometimes described as having a bushy habit. It can be difficult sometimes to distinguish between shrubs and trees. Some shrub species, such as *Magnolia*, *Rhododendron*, *Pittosporum*, *Parrotia* and *Ilex*, will eventually make immense specimens that because of their size, act like trees in the garden. However, because of their multiple stems, they will still usually be classified as shrubs. There are also some that remain compact but because they have a very clear upright shape act like small trees in the landscape. Sometimes they are called specimen shrubs. Plants such as *Cornus controversa* 'Variegata', *Aralia elata* and many of the dwarf maples make dramatically shaped specimen shrubs.

It can sometimes be difficult to know whether spiky plants are shrubs or not. Both *Yucca* and *Cordyline* are classified with shrubs as they will eventually produce a short woody trunk and, providing the winters are not too cold, will grow on to make substantial specimens. However, *Phormium*, the New Zealand flax, is an evergreen herbaceous perennial and not a shrub because it does not produce woody structures. This can be confusing as phormiums are often listed with shrubs in plant catalogues, which is incorrect, but most of them have as much impact in a garden as a shrub. Confusing!

There are also some plants that are referred to as subshrubs. These are generally low-growing plants that have a woody structure that is not totally permanent. So, for example, most *Euphorbias* produce strong shoots that are clothed with greyish-green leaves in their first year and in the second year go on to produce flowers and seeds. After this the stems die but there is a constant production of new stems each year from the base of the plant. From a horticultural point of view we usually treat these slightly differently, often by pruning out the dying wood after flowering each year.

OPPOSITE: The spiky-leaved *Yucca flaccida* 'Ivory' makes a handsome specimen plant especially when in bloom in midsummer.

Identifying shrubs: those terrible Latin names

You won't get far in this book, or almost any gardening book, without encountering botanical Latin. New gardeners often complain that they do not understand botanical names, and certainly they can be daunting. Some would argue that greater use should be made of common names but these are not precise. For example, the word 'daisy' could refer to any number of similar plants from the common lawn weed through to exotic plants such as the *Gerbera*, all of which have a similar multi-petalled form. The common name sycamore refers to three different trees depending on where you are! In the UK sycamore usually refers to *Acer pseudoplatanus*, a rather coarse weed tree, but in the USA it refers to *Platanus occidentalis*, the tree known in the UK as the London plane. Baffling? It is therefore well worth any gardener who has more than a cursory interest getting to understand how plants are properly named.

So here goes! Most plants will have two Latin names that give them their precise botanical name, sometimes called the binomial system. It is also called the Linnaean system, after the botanist Carl Linnaeus who first classified the plant kingdom in 1735. No other plant will have the same combination of names and this is recognizable by gardeners and botanists throughout the world, regardless of language,. Once you understand some botanical Latin, you can visit a botanic garden or nursery in any country and read the plant labels. For example:

Hydrangea macrophylla (common hydrangea).

The first word is the **genus** and is always spelt with a capital letter. The second word is the **species** and is spelt with a small letter. Both the genus and the species are usually printed in italic script in books. Now there are of course many different hydrangeas and so we can also have:

Hydrangea macrophylla 'Endless Summer', like all blue hydrangeas, needs an acid soil to maintain its vivid blue flowers.

Hydrangea arborescens
Hydrangea paniculata
Hydrangea quercifolia

The species word is a describing word and tells us a bit about the type of hydrangea: so, quite simply, *macrophylla* means large-flowered, *arborescens* means tree-like, *paniculata* means flowers in panicles, whereas *quercifolia* tells us the plant has leaves that resemble those of an oak tree (*Quercus*). Species names are quite useful in that they often tell us about the conditions the plant needs or about how it is going to perform in the garden.

SOME USEFUL SPECIES NAMES

horizontalis	spreading
nana	dwarf
sempervirens	evergreen
floribunda	free-flowering
grandiflora	large-flowered
argentea	silvery
rubra	red
lutea	yellow
foetida	strong-smelling
odorata	sweet-scented
praecox	early-flowering
hookerii	named after Sir Joseph Hooker
capensis	of the Cape, i.e. South Africa
aquatica	growing by water
sylvestris	of woodland origin

Plants with two Latin names are all natural forms that have originated in the wild. Some plants have a third name such as *Hydrangea quercifolia* 'Snow Queen'. This is a **cultivar** name and refers to a cultivated variety, which means that it originated in cultivation, possibly a garden or nursery, rather than in the wild. It will usually be an improvement on the wild species. Cultivar names are always given capital letters, enclosed with single quotes and are not in italic type. Sometimes in the nursery trade and garden centres this will be abbreviated to just the genus and cultivar. So you will see *Hydrangea* 'Snow Queen', *Choisya* 'Sundance' and *Camellia* 'Donation' for popular plants, which is quite acceptable as there is unlikely to be any confusion. Cultivar names are usually in the language of the country in which the plant originated but are often translated when a plant is imported. So *Bergenia* 'Abendglut' is often sold in the UK as *Bergenia* 'Evening Glow'.

Hybrids are crosses between two plants that have either been made deliberately or have occurred naturally, and when this happens you may see an × in a plant name. So the excellent winter-flowering shrub *Mahonia* × *media* 'Char-

Hydrangea paniculata 'Wim's Red' is an interesting example of this species, particularly grown for its contrasting red stems.

ity' is a hybrid from a cross between *M. japonica* and *M. lomarifolia*. When the × appears *before* the genus it refers to an intergeneric hybrid, which is less common; so you might find × *Mahoberberis aquisargentii*, which is a cross between a *Berberis* and a *Mahonia*.

Many people use the word **variety** when they really mean cultivar. A true variety is a variation on the basic form that has occurred in the wild. Continuing our example with *Choisya*, we have *Choisya dumosa* var *arizonica*, a wild collected plant mainly of botanical interest as one of the parents of *Choisya* 'Aztec Pearl'. A variety name has all lower case letters and no quotes.

Plant Breeders' Rights

Plant naming is never simple, and in recent years there has been the additional confusion of Plant Breeders' Rights, or Plant Patents as they are known in the USA. This is a registration that the raisers of new plants can make to protect their new introductions and ensure that they are always correctly labelled, and through which they receive a royalty payment. Often such plants will have a registered cultivar name and also a seller's name which is simply a name to appeal to gardeners when the plants are promoted and sold. So, for example, we have *Choisya ternata* 'Lich', more correctly and generally known as *Choisya* 'Sundance'. Easy, isn't it! In the chapter on new plants you will find a lot of these registered names correctly listed alongside the selling names. But for the sake of simplicity in this book, the most generally known names will be used as cultivar names even if this is botanically incorrect (I hope taxonomists will forgive me!).

Hardiness

You will also come across references to hardiness, which is a difficult subject about which to be precise. A particularly desirable plant may be hardy in one garden but repeatedly die over winter in nearby gardens. This can be due to any number of local factors, such as microclimate, aspect, soil, drainage, shelter and so on. So any recommendations can only be generalizations.

Although correctly known as 'Lich', this golden-leaved form of *Choisya ternata* is more regularly sold under the selling name of *Choisya* 'Sundance'.

Within our selection of plants in Chapter 5, you will see zone ratings with a number after the individual plant listings. These refer to a hardiness system developed in the USA and based on annual minimum temperatures for certain areas, called zones. Zone 1 is the coldest zone and Zone 11 the warmest. Plants are rated with the lowest zone in which they are likely to survive over winter. So if a plant is listed as a zone 8 plant it is likely also to survive in the warmer zone 9 but not in the cooler zone 7 or lower. This system is now being recognized and used outside the USA.

The UK is a small island and does not have great differences of climate, so it generally experiences conditions between zones 7 to 9. The majority of the country is zone 8, with the north of Scotland in zone 7, whereas the south west, parts of southern Ireland and other coastal areas are zone 9. Much of Europe spans zones 7 to 10. Detailed maps of the climate zones of all parts of the world are available on the internet.

The hardiness ratings quoted are based on those generally documented by other books and catalogues. For some unknown reason, the Royal Horticultural Society has developed its own hardiness ratings and these are loosely compared below.

The 'Totally Hardy' plants should survive almost anywhere and all winters in temperate areas. 'Generally Hardy' plants are also tough and should survive most areas and all but extreme winters. Plants listed as 'Borderline Hardy' are the gambles and may or may not survive a temperate winter depending on your local conditions.

Native or exotic

Plants are correctly described as native or exotic. Native plants are those that naturally grow in a certain area, whereas exotic plants are those that have originated from another country and been imported to grow in our gardens. (The word exotic is also popularly used to describe plants that have a tropical or jungle-like appearance and so we have the whole world of exotic gardening.) There are actually very few shrubs that are genuinely native to the British Isles, probably no more than about fifteen, although there are a few more that are naturalized and have been added to the countryside many years ago. Our native shrubs

Totally Hardy	Zone 7	RHS H4	Tolerates −12°C to −18°C	(0°F to 10°F)
Generally Hardy	Zone 8	RHS H3-4	Tolerates −7°C to −12°C	(10°F to 20°F)
Borderline Hardy	Zone 9	RHS H3	Tolerates −1°C to −7°C	(20°F to 30°F

WINTER FATALITIES

During the time this book was being written, the UK experienced one of the harshest winters on record. Snow started falling in November 2010 and became widespread throughout December. Temperatures generally fell below −10°C and in certain areas as low as −21°C and it continued to be cold through January 2011, with further snowfalls in certain areas. The result in horticultural terms has been the death of numerous plants generally thought to be hardy. Ceanothus, Hebe, Cordyline, Phormium and many other genera have died, although some may regenerate from their roots. Despite the disappointment and cost, it has to be said that this was an exceptional winter. December was the coldest since records began in 1910, breaking the previous coldest record of 1981. As information on survivors and losses are correlated, the Royal Horticultural Society is rewriting their hardiness ratings with a revised scale and it is intended to encourage UK gardeners and plant retailers to adopt this new system.

Euonymus europaeus **is a native of the United Kingdom and has brilliant pink and orange fruits as well as its colourful autumn foliage.**

become safety hazards, blocking sight lines near roads, creating dark places and compromising personal safety. Inevitably they are hard pruned. The effect is lost and a permanent maintenance problem has been created. Also, being totally blunt, most natives have very limited ornamental value – they are unlikely to win awards at your local flower show!

ORIGIN OF SHRUBS

Over the years, many exotic plants have been introduced from far-flung parts of the world and, amazingly, grow and thrive in our temperate climate. Despite what is said about the weather in the United Kingdom, it is in fact ideal for creating gardens and growing an immense range of plants. Although the UK experiences frost and sometimes snow, winter temperatures are rarely excessively cold and many plants will tolerate this. Severe heat and drought are rare, summers are mild and the rain that is so often cursed provides an ideal environment for establishment and growth. Because of this the UK is rightly famous for its beautiful gardens and extensive plant collections.

The earliest plant introductions were either food plants such as grapevines and medlars, introduced by the Romans, or incidental introductions brought back by those travelling for various other reasons. A few plants such as lavender, rosemary and the Gallica rose were introduced as early as the thirteenth and fourteenth centuries. One of the first dedicated plant hunters was John Tradescant the younger. The genus *Tradescantia* is named after his father, also a plant hunter called John Tradescant. The son, however, travelled to North America in 1628 and sent back a variety of plants including Virginia creeper, magnolias and many big trees such as *Liriodendron*, the tulip tree. However, it was during the eighteenth and nineteenth centuries, the era of the great plant hunters, that so many new plants, including trees and shrubs, were first imported into the United Kingdom.

are actually quite a plain bunch and include plants such as holly, dogwood, spindle, elder, box, buckthorn, grey willow and blackthorn.

In recent years there has been a great deal of emphasis on the use of native plants in landscape schemes. Such schemes are deemed environmentally sensitive and commended for supporting wildlife. However, whilst on the surface this would seem highly laudable, such schemes are not without problems. Most native shrubs are vigorous plants and when planted in inappropriate landscape schemes such as near buildings, alongside footpaths and around car parks, they soon become problem plants. Tall plants such as these

Most early plant introductions were by seed, as

The bottlebrush plant, *Callistemon rigidus*, originates from Australia, so is technically an exotic plant but is virtually hardy in the UK.

TIME LINE: UK PLANT INTRODUCTIONS

Lavandula angustifolia (lavender)	1265	*Forsythia suspensa*	1833
Rosmarinus officinalis (rosemary)	1340	*Weigela florida*	1845
Cistus salviifolius	1548	*Mahonia bealei*	1849
Salvia officinalis (sage)	1597	*Griselinia littoralis*	1850
Rhus typhina	1629	*Hamamelis mollis*	1879
Ruta gravaeolens (rue)	1652	*Buddleja davidii*	1890
Hypericum calycinum	1676	*Pieris formosa var forrestii*	1905
Camellia japonica	1739	*Hydrangea macrophylla*	1917
Cornus alba	1741	*Mahonia lomarifolia*	1931
Aucuba japonica	1783	*Paeonia lutea var ludlowii*	1947
Fuchsia magellanica	1788	*Callistemon pallidus*	1984
Choisya ternata	1825	*Schefflera taiwaniana*	2003
Wisteria floribunda	1830	*Hydrangea longifolia*	2009

live plants had a very low rate of survival. Travel was by sea, the voyages were long, and plants died either from lack of light in a ship's hold or from salt spray if kept on deck. All that was revolutionized in the middle of the nineteenth century as the result of an invention by Dr Nathaniel Ward. He was a naturalist and used a glass case to rear butterflies. He observed that small ferns grew and thrived in this case much more successfully than those outdoors, where they struggled against city air pollution. In 1833 he had some glass cases constructed and despatched plants in them to Australia; they arrived in excellent condition, as did the return consignment. A Wardian case, as it became known, was simply a small enclosed and sealed glasshouse. As plants grow, their own moisture is recycled. Plants could then be sent on deck, protected within their glass cases and able to utilize the sun for growth on the long journey home.

The plant hunters

Plant hunting was an expensive exercise and so was usually sponsored either by botanic gardens and commercial nurseries or by wealthy landowners with a particular interest in plants. Amongst the many names, certain people stand out because of their great success in sending back plants that have now become key components of our gardens. **Robert Fortune** was sent out to China by the Horticultural Society (later the Royal Horticultural Society) in 1842 and subsequently to Taiwan and Japan. He sent back over 190 different species of plants such as jasmine, *Weigela* and *Forsythia*, which are now common in our gardens. He is commemorated by *Trachycarpus fortunei* and *Euonymus fortunei*, both named after him. He died in 1880.

   Sir Joseph Dalton Hooker was a botanist and close friend of Darwin. In 1847 he left for

Wardian cases, like this example, revolutionized the transport of new plant introductions in the middle of the nineteenth century.

a three-year expedition to India and the Himalayas, which resulted in the introduction of many plants, particularly rhododendrons. He is also commemorated by one of his own introductions, *Crinodendron hookerianum*, a slightly tender shrub with beautiful red flowers. He succeeded his father William Hooker as director of Kew Gardens in 1865.

During the nineteenth century, the largest European nursery was a firm based in Exeter and Chelsea, known as James Veitch & Son. They were the first commercial nursery to sponsor their own plant collectors, employing over twenty-two collectors who were sent to many countries over a period of seventy-two years. Many famous names appear in their list of plant collectors. Over that period of time they introduced over 1,281 new plants, including 153 trees, shrubs and woody climbers as well as many herbaceous plants, bulbs and tender greenhouse plants. Amongst the shrubs of interest to us here are plants such as *Abutilon vitifolium*, *Berberis darwinii*, *Ceanothus* × *veitchianus*, *Cotoneaster dammeri*, *Deutzia gracilis*, *Hydrangea macrophylla* 'Veitchii', *Magnolia stellata*, *Sarcococca humilis* and *Viburnum davidii*, all very familiar plants in our modern garden centres. It is strange to think of them as novelties.

Amongst the collectors that the Veitches employed was **Ernest 'Chinese' Wilson**, as he became known. He went out to China in 1901 and in a period of only one year sent back seeds of 671 different species, including *Berberis wilsoniae*, *Actinidia chinensis*, *Ilex pernyi*, *Clematis montana* var *rubens* and *Kolkwitzia amabilis*. Over sixty species of plant bear his name. Many of the original plants can still be seen at Caerhays Castle in Cornwall, such as specimens of *Magnolia sargentiana* and *Rhododendron fargesii*.

Abutilon vitifolium, a vigorous but tender wall shrub, was originally collected for the Veitches by William Lobb in Chile and introduced in 1842.

Many of the mature rhododendrons in Sheringham Park, Norfolk, originate from Ernest Wilson's nineteenth-century plant hunting trips to China.

George Forrest was working in the early twentieth century and was sent out to China by the Edinburgh Botanic Gardens. Altogether he made six expeditions and discovered over 1,200 plants new to science. Gardeners can thank him for *Pieris forrestii, Mahonia lomarifolia, Rhododendron sinogrande* and numerous species of *Buddleja, Deutzia, Berberis, Cotoneaster* and conifer. He also sent plants back to Caerhays Castle, including *Camellia saluensis* in 1924; this was one of the parents of *Camellia × williamsii* and all the subsequent hybrids that are now so widely grown. Around 1905, George Forrest barely escaped with his life while in China, travelling by night and hiding by day, and enduring near-starvation while dodging hunting parties of warrior priests scouring the countryside for victims. Despite this he carried on plant hunting!

It is easily forgotten what arduous expeditions these people undertook, often lasting several years and without any modern convenience or support. Many plant hunters suffered considerable hardships, risks, illnesses and life-threatening incidents, all in the cause of discovering new plants for gardens back in the UK. In 1910 Ernest Wilson was working in the Min Valley when his leg was crushed during an avalanche as he was carried along the trail in his sedan chair. After setting his leg with the tripod of his camera, he was carried back to civilization. Then there was **David Douglas**, who went out three times to North America and introduced some 240 new species, including many fine trees. Sadly he died in Hawaii, having fallen into a pit trap where he was gored to death by a bull. He was buried in an unmarked grave in Honolulu, Hawaii.

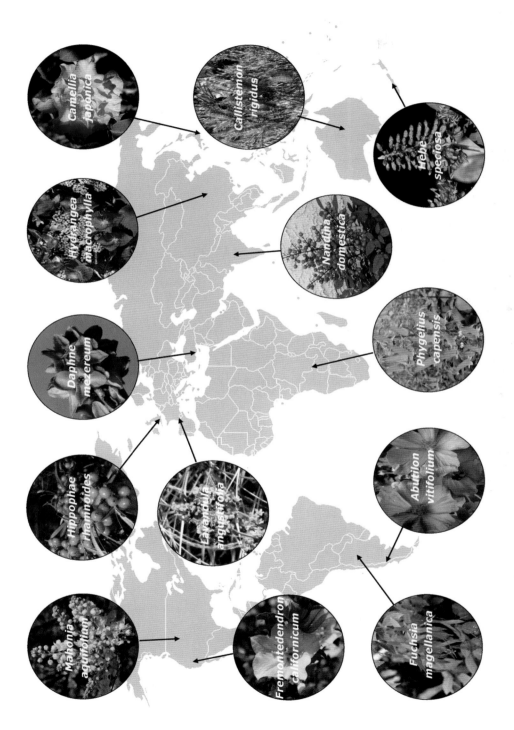

Amazingly, there are shrubs from every continent that will grow and thrive in the temperate climate of the United Kingdom.

Schefflera macrophylla, **introduced from Taiwan by the Wynn Joneses in 2003, is a spectacular foliage shrub but needs a sheltered location.**

Modern Plant Hunting

Although so much of the world has been explored and thousands of plants introduced, there are still curious horticulturalists and gardeners who have a fascination for the new and unknown. Amazingly, there are still plants out there in the wilds that have not been recorded or introduced to cultivation and so there continue to be plant hunters who scour the world for new introductions. Despite modern technology and the relative ease of modern travel compared to the nineteenth century, plant hunting is still a demanding and arduous process. Before even booking flights, it is essential to secure the appropriate government licences for visiting remote areas and collecting plants and seeds. In some ways it's even more complex today than it was for the early plant hunters!

Bleddyn Wynn Jones and wife Sue own Crûg Farm Plants, a nursery and garden in north Wales. Each year since 1991 they have ventured abroad on a plant hunting expedition, visiting many countries in the Far East, Middle East, South America and Asia. Their huge nursery list shows many plants that they have introduced to cultivation. Their nursery catalogue is a fascinating source of information about the plants they have collected and their origins. Possibly one of the most astonishing is the recently introduced *Schefflera macrophylla* BSWJ9788, collected from Northern Vietnam in 2003. The leaves are huge and handsome, comprised of five leaflets on delicate leaf stalks. When the young leaves emerge they are velvety with an attractive cinnamon colouring that matures to deep green.

Michael Wickenden of Cally Gardens has been making expeditions since 1987 and brought back seed of a number of wild collected species. Tony Schilling was in charge of the gardens at Wakehurst Place for many years and made trips to the Himalayas, where he collected many species. Roy Lancaster is probably best known as a captivating speaker and gardening writer with an abundant enthusiasm for plants. Over the years he has also travelled extensively in many countries, sometimes retracing the routes of Victorian plant hunters. He has been a member of expeditions to Nepal and Yunnan, China, and has published accounts of both in his books *A Plantsman in Nepal* and *Travels in China*. In 1999 he was awarded the OBE for his services to horticulture.

NINETEENTH-CENTURY GARDENS

The nineteenth century was the heyday of horticulture, and Victorian gardeners welcomed the influx of new plants. This stimulated a particular approach to garden design, aimed at showcasing new introductions. This style included winding paths through grassy areas with scattered plantings of individual shrubs, as well as island beds. Although informal, there was no attempt to mimic nature and the layouts were distinctly contrived to highlight botanical curiosity and the beauty of special plants. Sometimes there would be an emphasis on the origin of the plants so we find references to American, Chinese or Japanese gardens. The style was known as Gardenesque and particular proponents of this were the horticulturalist John Claudius Loudon and the landscape designer Humphrey Repton.

The garden around the Royal Pavilion in Brighton is a reconstruction that aims to show the sort of Gardenesque landscapes in vogue in the middle of the nineteenth century.

Later in the nineteenth century, the use of more closely planted shrubs developed and became known as a shrubbery. Plants were massed together, with elements of contrast and variety built in for interest. Shrubberies were usually arranged around winding gravel pathways that made a circuitous tour around the garden, offering the opportunity for exercise and private conversation. It was very much a feature of English gardens surrounding suburban villas.

A good example of a shrubbery is in the restored garden at the Royal Pavilion Brighton, originally an extravagant residence built by the Prince of Wales, later King George IV. Much of the shrubbery planting is based on 'rules' for the design of shrubberies described in 1828 by Henry Phillips, a local landscape gardener. Phillips advises that 'a well-planted shrubbery depends on the selection of trees and shrubs which succeed each other in blossoming throughout the year, as well as contrasting shades of green for permanent effect and under-planted flowers for the shorter duration'.

These Victorian styles survive in many of our traditional city parks, which were originally developed in the nineteenth century. Botanic gardens, in which the emphasis on individual plants remains a high priority, also continue to display plants in a conventional way.

TWENTIETH-CENTURY NURSERYMEN

There are, of course, many nurseries and nurserymen that have dominated the plant production scene during the twentieth century but three firms stand out as being particularly significant.

Waterers

In 1829 Michael Waterer, together with his brother John and three sons, took over an existing nursery at Bagshot in Surrey. They worked the nursery, specializing in American plants and, particularly, rhododendrons, which thrived on the acid sandy soil. By 1870 they were the largest nursery in the area, with 60 acres of rhododendrons. They were responsible for a number of introductions, including the hybrid rhododendron 'Pink Pearl'. Whilst on trial, this new cultivar disappeared but was discovered in an employee's garden and returned to the nursery. It received an award of merit in 1897 and has become one of the most popular rhododendrons of all time. Waterers were one of the first nurseries to start growing plants in containers, initially tin cans, an idea imported from American nurseries which in time led to modern container growing. From 1951 the nursery specialized in *Rhododendron yakushimanum* hybrids, which are compact and free-flowering cultivars particularly suitable for modern gardens.

Notcutts

Notcutts nurseries developed from the family business of John Woods when it was sold to Roger Crompton Notcutt in 1897. The business started with 11 acres of land but more was soon added and a retail shop opened in nearby Woodbridge in 1913. In the early years the business concentrated on supplying plants to some of the great houses and gardens in the country, although this business declined after the First World War. Plants were delivered initially by horse and cart and later by lorry or rail. Notcutts were responsible for the introduction of several specific cultivars such as *Cotinus coggygria* 'Notcutts' Variety', *Hibiscus syriacus* 'Woodbridge' and *Viburnum* × *bodnantense* 'Deben'. It was one of the first nurseries to develop a purpose-built garden centre, the first of which opened in Woodbridge in 1958. Now they own nineteen garden centres. Waterers nurseries were purchased by Notcutts in 1982, giving them the soil and expertise to grow a wider range of rhododendrons and ericaceous plants. In 1985 Notcutts acquired Mattocks Roses, adding further to the range of plants grown by the nursery. Over the years Notcutts has exhibited at many flower shows, including Chelsea, and been awarded over 50 gold medals. However, in 2007 Notcutts

The Sir Harold Hillier Gardens contain over 12,000 different species of trees and shrubs planted throughout 72 hectares (180 acres) of landscaped gardens.

Nurseries was purchased through a management buyout, taking history full circle with the re-establishment of the name John Woods Nurseries. Notcutts continue to be active as garden centre operators.

Hilliers

Of the three nurseries described, Hilliers is prob- ably the most famous, although it started in a small way with 2 acres purchased by Edwin Hillier in the 1860s. A further 130 acres were added in 1883. Harold Hillier joined the business in 1921 and it is during his era that the business really developed, with an ideal mix of skilled plants- manship and good business sense. Much of the business was mail order in the era of cheap post- age. Many important customers were supplied

National Collections, like this one of *Buddleja*, aim to grow as many different species and cultivars of one genus as possible, side by side for comparison.

and in 1935 Hilliers achieved the Royal Warrant for supplying the royal household. In 1953 Harold Hillier purchased Jermyns, near Braishfield in Hampshire, as his private residence and started developing his own arboretum. This was eventually given to Hampshire County Council in 1977, opened to the public and today is one of the primary collections of trees and shrubs in the UK. Hilliers opened garden centres from the 1960s and particularly developed a wholesale market for shrubs and large trees from the 1970s. In 1972 the first edition of *The Hillier Manual of Trees and Shrubs* was printed, now accepted as one of the primary reference works for woody plants in temperate areas. Harold Hillier was knighted for his services to horticulture in 1983. Over the years Hilliers have exhibited at many shows and in 2010 received their sixty-first consecutive Gold Medal for their Chelsea flower show entry.

Plant Conservation

With the increasing destruction of many wild habitats, there has been concern for many years about the loss of plant species. Botanic gardens are often linked with universities and their primary purpose is normally research, education and conservation. Horticultural display and visitor facilities are usually secondary, although often essential for financial security. In recent years the conservation of wild species has become increasingly important. Many botanic gardens concentrate only on wild collected species and each institute may have a particular specialism. Worldwide there are probably around 1,800 botanic gardens in 150 countries. There is a network among botanic gardens and an exchange of seed aids in the conservation of plants. All very efficient!

Some years ago, it was recognized that there was little co-ordinated conservation for garden plants and many old and unusual plants were being lost or threatened. From this grew an organization that started in 1978 as the National Council for the Conservation of Plants and Gardens, more recently renamed Plant Heritage. This organization oversees the conservation of garden plants in the UK, particularly old cultivars. This is done by means of National Collections, of which there are currently around 650. Most National Collections are based on a single genus and may be held by an individual with a particular interest or by an organization or commercial nursery. Collections may be in nurseries, large estates or just small private gardens.

Any individual can start to develop a collection of a favourite plant and, if they feel they have a substantial collection, apply for it to be given national status. Although some support is available, collection holders are very much independent. Maintaining records of a substantial plant collection, as well as looking after them, can be an arduous task, which means that most of the larger collections are held by organizations that have support resources. For example, the National Collection of *Hydrangea* is held by Derby City Parks and displayed in an old walled garden in Darley Abbey Park. There are 470 different species and cultivars in the collection. The Royal Horticultural Society gardens hold collections of *Cornus, Viburnum, Ilex* and heathers. By contrast the National Collection of *Euphorbia*, amounting to over 143 species and cultivars, is held by one enthusiastic amateur gardener and mainly grown on his allotment.

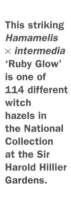
This striking *Hamamelis × intermedia* 'Ruby Glow' is one of 114 different witch hazels in the National Collection at the Sir Harold Hillier Gardens.

2 THE SHRUB REPERTOIRE

So what is it that makes shrubs such a valuable group of plants? Initially, there are just so many of them that there really is a shrub for almost every situation, whether it be sun or shade, wet or dry, clay soil or sandy. And then it's what they have to offer to your garden. There are shrubs that will give you coloured foliage, flowers, scent, winter stems, interesting shapes and a whole host of other benefits. And in the wonderful world of shrubs, you can find plants that are of interest during the full twelve months of the year, including right through the dreariest days of winter.

FLOWERING SHRUBS

Walk round any garden centre or public garden and it will probably be flowering shrubs that first catch your eye. Visiting a garden such as the Savill Gardens in Windsor Great Park during the spring, nobody can fail to be impressed by the dazzling colour. The thousands of rhododendrons in bloom at this time make an unrivalled show of colour. Continue to visit in the summer, autumn and winter and there will still be other flowering shrubs to enjoy.

Flowering shrubs come in every conceivable colour: yellow *Potentilla,* blue *Ceanothus,* pink *Cistus,* red *Chaenomeles,* orange *Rhododendron,* white *Philadelphus* and purple *Syringa.* There is even a new *Hydrangea* called 'Limelight' with unique green blooms that mature to a rich autumnal pink. The display from flowering shrubs may

OPPOSITE: *Clerodendron bungei* is a suckering shrub that flowers in late summer so can be cut back hard each spring.

come either from hundreds of tiny flowers packed together, on plants such as *Ceanothus,* or from the single impressive blooms of plants such as *Magnolia grandiflora* 'Exmouth', whose individual flowers can be over 20cm (9in) in diameter.

Traditionally many shrubs were vigorous and made big plants, but modern cultivars of so many shrubs are compact and much more suitable for small gardens. For example, the old *Philadelphus* 'Virginal' makes a 3m (10ft) tall plant covered in white scented flowers – spectacular if you have the space. However, in most gardens the compact 'Manteau d'Hermine', which grows to 90cm (3ft) and also has white scented flowers, may be far more suitable. Do look for modern compact cultivars if space is an issue.

A high proportion of flowering shrubs are at their peak in spring and early summer. We have already mentioned the huge range of rhododendrons but there are many others, some familiar, such as the classic lilac, and other less common, such as the exquisite *Carpenteria californica* with beautiful snowy white flowers and golden stamens. Don't ignore common genera such as *Potentilla.* There are so many good cultivars with flowers in yellows, oranges, white and pink, and most of them have a very long flowering season. As summer progresses, there are many more shrubs with a late summer fanfare including a host of *Buddleja, Escallonia,* hardy *Fuchsia* and an array of blue-flowered shrubs including *Cerastostigma, Perovskia, Caryopteris* and *Ceanothus* 'Gloire de Versailles'.

Some plants bear catkins, which are slim, usually cylindrical, clusters of flowers, often without petals, that are usually wind-pollinated. They are often unisexual and so you will find both male and female catkins separately on a shrub. The

Mahonias are evergreen shrubs that occasionally exhibit vivid leaf colour; this usually signals a serious leaf drop on parts of the plant.

males are often the showy ones! Willows have catkins as do the hazels. One of the best is *Corylus maxima* 'Purpurea', with purple foliage, reddish catkins and a red husk around the fruit. *Garrya elliptica* is an excellent evergreen for a north wall, producing long, trailing, tassel-like catkins in silvery grey that last throughout the winter. The desirable cultivar 'Glasnevin Wine' has ruby-red catkins, well worth searching out. Rather than flowers, a few plants have bracts: coloured leaves which have the appearance of flowers. The limey-green heads of *Euphorbia* are made up of colourful bracts, as are the shiny red parts of the *Leycesteria* flower.

Winter flowering shrubs

Although not the peak season for flowering shrubs, your garden need not be without colour

WINTER FLOWERING SPECIES

AGM after a plant indicates that it has received the Royal Horticultural Society's recommendation, the Award of Garden Merit.

Name	Description	Height
Chimonanthus praecox AGM	Deciduous, sweetly scented yellow flowers	1.8m (6ft)
Daphne mezereum	Deciduous shrub, pink flowers, poisonous	90cm (3ft)
Daphne bholua 'Jane Postil' AGM	Scented pink and white flowers, midwinter	90cm (3ft)
Erica carnea cultivars	Heathers, pink and white, spreading, evergreen	1.8m (6ft)
Garrya elliptica 'James Roof' AGM	Evergreen wall shrub, silver tassels in winter	3m (10ft)
Hamamelis mollis AGM	Witch hazel, yellow flowers, autumn colour	2.1m (7ft)
Jasminum nudiflorum AGM	Sprawling climber, yellow flowers, all winter	4m (13ft)
Lonicera x purpusii 'Winter Beauty'	Small white flowers, rich honeysuckle scent	1.5m (5ft)
Mahonia 'Winter Sun' AGM	Evergreen, yellow flowers, fragrant	1.8m (6ft)
Skimmia japonica 'Rubella' AGM	Evergreen, spikes, red buds, white flowers	90cm (3ft)
Viburnum × bodnantense 'Dawn' AGM	Deciduous shrub, pink flowers	1.5m (5ft)
Viburnum tinus 'Eve Price' AGM	Easy evergreen, red buds, white flowers	2.1m (7ft)

in the winter and there are many shrubs worth growing to brighten up the long dull days between autumn and spring. Probably some of the first to come into flower are members of the genus *Mahonia*. Look out for 'Charity', 'Winter Sun' or 'Lionel Fortescue', all of which are similar. These are all hybrids from *M. japonica* and the slightly tender *M. lomariifolia*. Sometime around early winter, as the weather chills, they will start to open clusters of long racemes, packed with small yellow flowers, all sweetly scented and reminiscent of lily of the valley. The winter flowering heathers, cultivars of *Erica carnea*, are wonderful winter flowering groundcover plants, blooming from late autumn through to spring in many shades of white, pink and red. Unlike other types of heather, they are tolerant of chalky soils and easy to grow. Buy a few plants and bulk up for a whole border. Soon after Christmas, you are likely to see the first fascinating little flowers on the

witch hazels: ragged little tufts of yellow strand-like petals with a wonderful sweet perfume. This is likely to be the readily available *Hamamelis mollis*. In addition there are various hybrids such as the sulphur yellow 'Pallida', the coppery orange 'Jelena', and 'Diane' with rich ruby red flowers, all forms of *H. × intermedia*, crosses between *H. japonica* and *H. mollis*. And as well as this welcome winter colour, all *Hamamelis* have great autumn tints.

Scented shrubs

Scent is always a bonus, particularly from shrubs that already have attractive flowers or interesting foliage. When designing with shrubs, try to position scented plants close to paths and paved areas where you can easily appreciate their perfume. Nothing is worse than a wonderfully scented 'Etoile de Hollande' rose at the back of a border,

Although not new, *Buddleja* 'Lochinch', with its soft grey foliage and sweetly scented vivid blue flowers, is well deserving of its AGM.

tantalizing you with just a hint of its rich sweet perfume.

Scented flowers are particularly abundant during the winter months, starting in late autumn with the hybrid *Mahonias* with their sweet lily of the valley scent. The delicate *Chimonanthus praecox*, sometimes aptly called wintersweet, is not a spectacular shrub but worth growing for its scent alone. The somewhat insignificant evergreen members of the genus *Sarcococca* should not be forgotten, their tiny white scented flowers giving them their common name of sweet box.

Early summer brings many more scented subjects, familiar plants such as lilac, *Philadelphus* (mock orange), *Choisya* (Mexican orange blossom), the honey scent of *Pittosporum* and, of course, many of the shrub roses. A few scented flowers are at their peak at night, such as the

The inky-black foliage of *Sambucus* 'Black Lace' provides an excellent foil for the buttery-yellow leaves of *Cotinus* 'Golden Spirit'.

tender *Brugmansias*. Place them near a seat to appreciate on a warm summer evening. Late summer brings a few more, some with a heady, almost pungent fragrance, such as cultivars of *Buddleja*, the climbing *Jasminum officinale* and the powerful, almost intoxicating bouquet from the flowers of *Cordyline australis*. With the latter, a little goes a long way!

FOLIAGE SHRUBS

Foliage is undoubtedly far more important in any garden design than flowers, which come and go. Foliage contributes to your garden for many months, and with evergreens for the whole year. Shrubs have a number of characteristics, the most basic being colour, texture and form. Colour is self-explanatory but does of course encompass the colour of leaves, berries and stems as well as flowers, all of which alter with the seasons. Colour is probably the least important characteristic, although even with green leaves there are many different shades. Texture and form need some explanation. Texture refers to the pattern made by a plant's leaves, and form is all about the shape of a plant, sometimes called its structure. You will learn more about these in Chapter 6, but for now it's worth just emphasizing that there is a whole world of variety amongst the different types of foliage, without even considering flowers or berries.

Coloured foliage

There are many shrubs with variegated or coloured foliage that will contribute considerable interest to a planting scheme. One of the most spectacular, but sadly expensive, is *Aralia elata* 'Variegata'. This has huge variegated compound leaves, made up of a number of leaflets prettily marked with white. It is slow growing but in time makes a striking specimen with gracefully tiered foliage that turns pink before dropping in autumn. There is also a golden variegated version. Both produce clusters of lacy white flowers but these are almost superfluous.

All gardeners know privet but few grow its classy cousin, *Ligustrum lucidum* 'Excelsum Superbum'. This is a tall evergreen with polished leaves, variegated with jazzy yellow margins. The cultivar 'Tricolor' has pink tips when the foliage is young. The variegated dogwoods such as *Cornus alba* 'Elegantissima' and *C. stolonifera* 'White Gold' are grown not only for their summer foliage but also for their coloured winter stems that are revealed when the leaves drop in the autumn. *Weigela florida* 'Monet' is grown for its pink-tinted, white variegated foliage and also for its ruby-red flowers produced in early summer. A great improvement on the older *W. florida* 'Variegata'. If you want particularly good value for money, try *Philadelphus coronarius* 'Variegata', which not only has strikingly variegated foliage but also white flowers which have a strong perfume. It is one of the few variegated shrubs which prefer to be planted in light shade, as the foliage will burn in full sunshine.

There are also many golden-leaved shrubs such as *Cotinus coggygria* 'Golden Spirit', a fairly new form of the well-known smoke bush grown mainly for its foliage. As such it will respond well to hard pruning in the spring, which will give strong and vigorous well-coloured growths.

Leycesteria formosa 'Golden Lanterns' is another recent introduction. This is a vigorous shrub that should be sited at the back of the border, with bright golden foliage brushed with bronze when young. Towards the end of the summer it produces drooping racemes of small white flowers encased in rich ruby-red bracts. Another plant with year-round interest is that relative of the raspberry, *Rubus cockburnianus* 'Goldenvale'. Throughout the summer it produces a mass of arching canes covered in clear yellow lacy foliage. In the autumn the leaves drop, revealing striking silvery-white canes that contribute to the garden throughout the winter. Plant against a dark background such as *Osmanthus heterophyllus* and prune it hard each spring, right back to ground level.

Don't forget the value of green in the garden. *Rhus typhina* 'Laciniata' is a fine-leaved form of the stag's horn sumac. It makes a large bush draped with finely cut soft green foliage and then topped in midsummer with bright red furry flowers that give it its common name. Most gardeners would think of growing peonies for their flowers but the woody *Paeonia lutea* var *ludlowii* is worth growing for its deeply divided green foliage. This tree peony also has bright yellow flowers and large seedpods that open to reveal glossy black seeds.

Cercis canadensis 'Forest Pansy' may eventually make a small tree but regular pruning ensures vigorous rich ruby-red foliage and a compact habit.

Staying with shades of green, *Fatsia japonica*, the false castor oil plant, is familiar but still dramatic, with large hand-shaped glossy green leaves. It is vigorous and so should be placed where it has room to develop and can be appreciated. This is an excellent hardy plant to give the exotic effect in a jungle garden. Well worth growing!

Plants with bronze, ruby or purple foliage are particularly useful in planting schemes as they can be mixed with most other colours and plants. They look particularly effective when contrasted with paler colours. Be careful, however, to use dark foliage in sunny locations, otherwise it tends to just look drab. One of the best dark-leaved plants to appear in recent years is *Sambucus nigra* 'Black Lace', with very delicate, finely cut almost ebony foliage and saucer-like racemes of tiny sugar pink

flowers. If you want to restrict its size, it can be pruned hard but you will then just get the foliage and not the flowers. There are several red-leaved forms of *Berberis thunbergii* such as Dart's Red Lady', 'Red Chief' and the very upright 'Helmond Pillar'. If you want spiky purple foliage, try *Cordyline* 'Purple Tower' or 'Red Star', both of which will look good as young plants and then eventually grow into large specimens. There are many cultivars of *Acer palmatum* that make excellent specimen shrubs or even small trees, among them the richly coloured 'Bloodgood' or the finely dissected, ruby-leaved 'Garnet'. Like all dwarf maples, they like light shade, should not be allowed to dry out and must avoid late frosts.

Although there are many shrubs with purple or bronze foliage, very few of them are evergreen, most being deciduous and dropping their leaves in the autumn. Among the few that do keep their leaves over winter, one of the best is *Pittosporum* 'Tom Thumb'. This makes a compact bun-shaped plant no more than 90cm (3ft) high, fairly slow growing and very well behaved. In recent years, various members of the genus *Loropetalum* have started being available. These compact evergreens are related to witch hazel and have pretty pink or white flowers. Several cultivars such as 'Fire Dance' and 'Plum Delight' have rich purple foliage, although this may turn temporarily green in hot weather. They need a warm sheltered location. *Ceanothus* 'Tuxedo' is a new introduction with deep chocolate leaves and lavender blue flowers. It is a strong-growing shrub and needs plenty of space.

A few shrubs produce new young growth that is brilliant red in colour, although this does fade with time. One of the best is *Photinia×fraseri* 'Red Robin', which in time makes a large evergreen and also produces white flowers. A new cultivar called 'Little Red Robin' is more compact. *Pieris* 'Forest Flame' has a similar pattern of growth, with narrow leaves that are bright red when first produced, but this plant is a little more challeng-

Pieris formosa var. *forrestii* 'Wakehurst' must have an acid soil but will reward you with glistening white spring flowers and vivid red new growth.

ing as it requires an acid soil to grow effectively. With both of these, the foliage fades to a uniform green by midsummer. *Leucothoe* 'Scarletta' is also worth growing for its rich ruby young growth, which turns green in summer and then bronze in winter.

Evergreens

Any plant which looks good for twelve months of the year has to be good value and there are many shrubs that are evergreen and contribute to your garden throughout the year. The obvious value is in the winter colour and interest but this does mean that the display does not alter throughout the year. Evergreens do of course lose old leaves at some stage in the year and the young ones sometimes change their appearance as they age, but most are essentially the same. Good planting schemes will have a mixture of evergreens and deciduous plants.

There are so many worthy evergreens that it is difficult to know which to highlight. *Rhamnus alaterna* 'Variegata' is an excellent tall evergreen shrub for the back of the border. It has small leaves that are beautifully marked and is tough and easy to grow. The foliage is useful for picking to use in floral decoration. At the other end of the scale there are many excellent low-growing forms of *Euonymus fortunei* that make excellent groundcover plants. 'Dart's Blanket' makes a very successful dark green carpet of foliage. One of the most colourful is a cultivar called 'Sunspot', with golden splodges on dark green leaves, and yellow stems. The genus *Griselinia* comes from New Zealand but is hardy in most areas, making a tough, wind-tolerant, medium-sized bush with glossy rounded leaves. 'Dixon's Cream'

The golden leaves of *Ilex* × *altaclarensis* 'Lawsoniana' are spineless and make an effective contrast to its red winter berries.

and 'Bantry Bay' are particularly attractive variegated forms with a generous splatter of creamy white in the centre of the leaf, feathering gently to the edge. *Elaeagnus* includes cultivars such as 'Limelight' and the well-known *E. pungens* 'Maculata', which are both tall, colourful evergreen shrubs. And of course there are all the many cultivars of *Ilex*, commonly known as holly. There are many different types, both gold and silver variegated, and many of them have the bonus of winter berries. *Ilex × altaclarensis* 'Golden King' is confusingly a female holly and will, if pollinated, bear red berries. And just to add the gender issues, 'Golden Queen' and 'Silver Queen', both forms of *Ilex aquifolium*, are males! So much for diversity!

Some of these evergreens are such good, tough and reliable shrubs that they are rather too widely

An odd shoot on this hard-pruned *Santolina chamaecyparissus* escaped the secateurs and is showing the typical small yellow flowers.

planted in public areas. In using them in private gardens, you risk creating plantings rather too similar to your supermarket car park. *Elaeagnus*, *Euonymus*, *Mahonia aquifolium*, *Cotoneaster* 'Coral Beauty', *Viburnum tinus* and *Lonicera* 'Baggeson's Gold' all suffer from over-use.

Among the evergreens there are also those plants that have silver foliage. Most of them originate from slightly warmer areas such as the Mediterranean, where water supplies are often limited and the silvery foliage helps the plant to survive. Lavenders need little introduction: often the classic ingredient of a cottage garden, they are equally happy in modern landscapes. There are many cultivars, although one of the best is 'Grosso', a strong grower with deep purple flowers that do not set seed. It was introduced in 1972 by Pierre Grosso, who grows lavender commercially for oil production in France. *Artemisia* 'Powis Castle' makes low-growing cushions of finely-cut silver foliage. Grow in a sunny, well-drained location and prune it hard in the spring to retain a compact, well-clothed plant. *Santolina* is also best grown in the same way. *Hebe pinguifolia* 'Pagei' is another excellent ground cover plant, hundreds of tiny bluish-grey leaves making tight little buns of silver. In late spring it produces a bonus of small pearly-white flowers.

Aromatic foliage

Aromatic shrubs are a little more subtle, as they only release their scented oils when you touch them or possibly in very warm conditions. For this reason they are best planted in a warm, sheltered location. Many of the plants we think of as herbs come into this category, such as the sages, cultivars of *Salvia officinalis* such as 'Purpurascens' with purple foliage, 'Icterina' with golden leaves, and the compact 'Tricolor' with its pretty white, purple and pink leaves. *Perovskia*, loved for its late summer blue flowers, has a similar sage smell. Then there are hundreds of ornamental thymes, different types of rosemary, sweet bay and, of course, traditional lavender in so many forms. *Ruta gravaeolens* 'Jackman's Blue', a good cultivar of the aromatic rue, has grey foliage which borders on blue. Don't forget that it is poisonous and contact with the foliage can cause skin irritation. The rock roses, members of the genus *Cistus*, have aromatic foliage, as does *Choisya* with its perfumed flowers, and not forgetting the sweet briar, *Rosa rubiginosa*. One more to mention is *Aloysia citriodora*, lemon verbena, a compact, somewhat tender and straggly plant with insignificant flowers but an astonishingly powerful lemon fragrance. Grow it in a pot and position near where you sit in your garden – wonderful!

Some aromatic foliage is an unexpected and not always pleasant surprise. The crushed leaves of *Clerodendron trichotomum* have an unfortunate but curious smell of burnt milk. Many conifers have a distinctive pungent smell, as does the so-called curry plant, *Helichrysum italicum*, smelling just like your local Indian take-away but having nothing whatsoever to do with Asian cookery! Plant *Melianthus major* where it can be seen but not touched, as the delicate silver foliage has an extremely foul smell! Finally, of course, there is the timeless smell of *Buxus sempervirens*, box hedging.

Autumn colour

Many people travel to the USA just to see the autumn colours in New England. And certainly many trees and shrubs can be spectacular with golds and reds before the leaves drop. Autumn tints are rarely as brilliant in the UK but there are nevertheless trees and shrubs worth planting for their autumn display. The development of autumn colour happens in response to shorter days and cooler temperatures. Chlorophyll, the green colouring in leaves, starts to break down, and two other sets of pigments, the carotenoids and the anthocyanins, become dominant, giving us the typical brilliant colourings from gold through orange and red to vivid purples. Despite the limitations, autumn colour can still often provide a wonderful finale for the summer border.

With some shrubs, autumn colour is a bonus above and beyond the main reason for growing them. *Hamamelis* has winter flowers, *Cotinus* has coloured summer foliage and *Euonymus europaeus* has coloured fruits, but all will also give us an extra display as their leaves prepare to drop for winter. Other shrubs such as *Fothergilla major*, *Parrotia*

Like most *Cotinus*, this bush of 'Golden Spirit' is showing some vivid autumn tints just before dropping its leaves.

persica and the dwarf maples are relatively plain for most of the season but suddenly become spectacular in the autumn with brilliant fiery sunset colours, making them well worth growing just for the short display.

BERRIES, SHAPE AND BARK

Flowers or colourful leaves are not the only reasons for growing plants and it is this great diversity that makes shrubs such interesting plants. In many cases shrubs will give more than one performance. So, for example, *Choisya* 'Aztec Pearl' has evergreen glossy leaves, white flowers and is scented; *Cornus alba* 'Aurea' has golden leaves, good autumn colour and red stems in winter. Such plants with a number of 'party tricks' are very good value and excellent constituents of a small garden.

Berries and fruits

Berried shrubs provide a garden with some very useful autumn colour that may be quite long-lived, although this will usually depend on the appetites of the local bird population. Sadly the flowers of many good foliage plants, such as *Pyracantha* and *Cotoneaster*, are insignificant. Shrub roses are the exception, usually having good flowers and often scent as well as colourful hips. Think of berries and most people would initially think

The evergreen *Nandina domestica*, sometimes called heavenly bamboo, produces white flowers and attractive winter berries.

of the colour red but the many berried garden plants include some that are available in a kaleidoscope of colours.

Botanically, not all the colourful fruits you may see in gardens are berries. The small aromatic, apple-like fruits of *Chaenomeles* are actually pomes, as are apples. *Hippophae*, the sea buckthorn, and *Elaeagnus* both produce drupes, and members of the genus *Rubus* produce compound fruits, like the related fruiting raspberry. But for garden purposes they can all be called berries. With a few species there is a two tone effect: the native shrub *Euonymus europaeus*, for example, has rosy red capsules that split open to reveal orange berries; 'Red Cascade' is a good garden cultivar. *Clerodendron trichotomum* has starry white flowers in pinkish calyces that are held after flowering, turning a rich ruby colour that contrasts vividly with the globular blue berries.

RAINBOW BERRIES	
Skimmia japonica	red
Pyracantha 'Orange Glow'	orange
Cotoneaster 'Rothschildianus'	yellow
Viburnum davidii	turquoise
Symphoricarpus albus	white
Gaultheria mucronata 'Lilian'	pink
Callicarpa 'Profusion'	purple
Clerodendron trichotomum	blue
Sarcococca confusa	black

Shape and specimen plants

Some plants are grown primarily for their shape and we have already encountered *Acer palmatum* cultivars and *Aralia elata* 'Variegata', both excellent specimen shrubs. Then there are the witch hazels, various types of *Hamamelis* that often make open, almost vase-shaped, plants and all look best grown on their own as features. The slow-growing *Viburnum plicatum* × *tomentosum* 'Mariesii' needs patience but will eventually produce a geometrically layered plant that in spring will be clothed in clusters of white lacecap flowers.

Some quite ordinary plants will produce great specimens if grown on their own and given enough space. For example, *Viburnum rhytidophyllum* is a vigorous leathery-leaved evergreen that is usually planted in far too little space and then hacked back to an ugly blob. Grow it as a lawn specimen, leave it alone and it will make a lovely, shapely round shrub, clothed in meticulously veined, leathery dark green leaves with abundant clusters of tiny white flowers in spring. *Pittosporum, Mahonia, Ilex* and the large cotoneasters such as 'Cornubia' will all make pleasing feature plants if given space to grow to their full potential.

It is difficult to know whether to include the magnolias. Although slow growing, many will eventually form small trees. The most familiar is *Magnolia* × *soulangeana*, a deciduous species with stunning white tulip-shaped flowers, tinted purple in spring. The cultivar 'Susan' is more compact, reaching only 2.1m (7ft) with beautiful reddish-violet buds opening to pale pink flowers. The best one for small gardens is *M. stellata*, the star magnolia, growing to around 1.2m (4ft). It

Cornus controversa 'Variegata' is grown for its stark architectural shape, making it an excellent specimen plant to be grown on its own.

produces masses of small white semi-double flowers with the bonus of scent. All of these will grow into excellent specimen plants, given space and time.

All spiky-leaved plants have strong shapes and some of the most dramatic are the yuccas from dry areas of North America, with huge sword-shaped leaves and towering flower spikes. *Yucca flaccida* 'Ivory' makes a chunky plant with pointed leaves ending in curling filaments. Each shoot flowers only once before dying but the flower is a spectacular towering spike of white bells. After flowering the main shoot is replaced by side shoots, although these may take several years to mature and flower. With or without flowers, yuccas make striking plants. The variegated types such as *Y. flaccida* 'Golden Sword' and *Y. gloriosa* 'Variegata' are well worth growing.

Coloured bark and curious stems

In the depths of winter, when the weather is cold and sharp frost has browned off the few intrepid winter flowers, you can still count on winter cheer from coloured stems and bark. Many of the species described provide an amazing amount of colour, which will absolutely glow in winter sunshine. The greatest contributors here are members of the genus *Cornus*, variations of the native dogwood. *Cornus alba* 'Sibirica' has green leaves and small white flowers that are followed by bluish-tinted berries. But it is in the winter that it is at its brightest, with brilliant lipstick-red wand-like twigs. There are also coloured-leaf versions such as 'Elegantissima' and 'Aurea' that also have red stems. For yellow stems you will need to grow *Cornus stolonifera* 'Flaviramea' or the variegated version 'White Gold'. There is also a cultivar called 'Midwinter Fire', which only has green leaves and so lacks interest in the summer, but is still well worth growing for its bright, fiery-orange stems. Site it towards the back of the border behind some deciduous plants and in winter, when its neighbours are leafless, its coppery stems will glow.

Some of the bushy willows will give a comparable display. *Salix alba vitellina* 'Britzensis' is sometimes called the scarlet willow for its brilliant winter stems; it looks good next to silvery-stemmed *Salix daphnoides* or the golden yellow *S. alba* var *vitellina*. All the dogwoods and willows are easy to grow and tolerant of waterlogged conditions.

The third genus that gives as good winter colour is *Rubus*, the same family as raspberries and blackberries. *Rubus cockburnianus* is a vigorous shrub producing huge arched thorny stems, so only plant it where you have sufficient space, or where you want a prickly barrier. Its value is seen in the winter when the leaves drop to reveal a fine tracery of delicate branches all covered with a chalky white coating. For a more compact version of this try *Rubus thibetanus* 'Silver Fern' or the colourful 'Goldenvale', which also has golden foliage. Another plant well worthy of inclusion here is *Perovskia atriplicifolia* 'Blue Spire',

Acer palmatum 'Sango-kaku' (syn 'Senkaki') looks particularly good in winter with its colourful naked stems dusted with snow.

Shrubs can do some strange things: this *Fuchsia magellanica* has grown up and through a golden conifer hedge.

grown primarily for its blue flowers, but it also has scented silvery-grey foliage and chalky white winter stems. For the best stem colour, you should hard prune all these at regular intervals.

There are a few shrubs with curious twisted stems, sometimes used for flower arranging. Probably the best known is *Corylus avellana* 'Contorta', the corkscrew hazel. The cultivar 'Red Majestic' also has wine-red leaves and ruby catkins. *Salix babylonica* var *pekinensis* 'Tortuosa', the corkscrew willow, has twisted yellow stems and will eventually make a small tree but can be kept at shrub size by hard spring pruning. The similar *Salix alba* 'Dart's Snake' has shiny black twisted stems and *Salix erythroflexuosa* has wavy coppery, almost red, stems. These shrubs are mostly unassuming in summer but reveal their bizarre skeletons when the leaves drop for winter.

Year-round colour

Gardens need never be without interest at any time of the year when you have a good selection of shrubs. With a combination of flowers, foliage, scent, berries and coloured stems there can be something to enjoy every day of the year.

FOUR SEASONS OF COLOUR

Spring	*Mahonia* × *wagneri* 'Undulata' – evergreen plus golden yellow flowers
	Viburnum burkwoodii - round heads of sweetly scented white flowers
	Ribes speciosum – glossy foliage, red, fuchsia-like pendant flowers
Summer	*Berberis* × *stenophylla* – masses of scented golden yellow flowers
	Choisya 'Aztec Pearl' – aromatic evergreen foliage, scented white flowers
	Cytisus praecox 'Albus' – Warminster broom, silky shoots, white pea-like flowers
Autumn	*Ceanothus* 'Gloire de Versailles' – Californian lilac, masses of sky blue flowers
	Indigofera heterantha – unusual shrub with racemes of delicate purple flowers
	Pyracantha 'Orange Glow' – evergreen, reliable, huge bunches of orange berries
Winter	*Chimonanthus praecox* – wintersweet, small claw-like scented yellow flowers
	Cornus 'Midwinter Fire' – glowing orange winter stems plus autumn tints
	Hamamelis mollis 'Pallida' – witch hazel, sulphur-yellow tufted flowers, scent

3 RIGHT SHRUB, RIGHT PLACE

Among the thousands of shrubs available, there really are plants for every location imaginable: different soils, warm and sheltered gardens, or cold and exposed locations. There are also shrubs for almost any purpose you could imagine: for covering walls or trellises, for groundcover, to grow in containers, for architectural effect and even to act as burglar deterrents! Success depends very much on choosing the right plant for the right place, so if you have a tricky situation or a particular need, do take the time to find out what shrubs are likely to flourish for you.

SHRUBS FOR A LOCATION

Far too often, gardeners act on impulse and buy an attractive plant, only to get it home and wonder where to plant it. (We all do it!) Too often it ends up in whatever gap is available, regardless of its suitability, and twelve months later they will be asking why it didn't grow. Matching the right plant to the right place initially goes a long way towards success.

Hot, dry conditions

You may dream of gardening in a warm climate, where there is plenty of sunshine and it's always warm. However, in a temperate climate even the most average garden will usually have at least one little hotspot, where the sun bakes the soil and it's always warm and well drained. This is the location where you can grow a selection of plants that revel in such hot, dry conditions.

Try growing the brightly coloured *Cistus* such as the brilliant cerise 'Sunset', the compact 'Grayswood Pink' with pale pink flowers and silvery foliage, or the tough white *C. × corbariensis*, and they will reward you with numerous colourful summer flowers like crumpled paper tissues. All the different species and cultivars of *Ceanothus*, originally from California, thrive in hot, dry conditions. Most flower in shades of blue, although there are one or two white and pink types. There are many different species and cultivars, from the almost prostrate and rather tender *C. gloriosus* up to the almost tree proportions of the superb 'Trewithen Blue' that is rarely without flower. By all means try *Ceanothus thyrsiflorus* 'Repens', which is a very free-flowering plant – but beware of its confusing name, which means creeping but goes with a bush that may be as much as 2.1m (7ft) high. *Romneya coulteri* is a member of the poppy family originating from California and thriving in hot, dry locations. It can be slow to establish but once settled will thrill you with huge white, sweetly scented flowers with golden stamens. Beware though: it suckers if very content! Members of the pea family such as yellow-flowered *Genista*, tall yellow *Spartium junceum*, the less common pink-flowered *Indigofera heterantha*, as well as all the many different coloured *Cytisus*, will all thrive in hot, dry, baked conditions.

And to go with all that colour add some silver foliage such as *Artemisia* 'Powis Castle', *Phlomis fruticosa*, *Santolina chamaecyparissus*, or maybe the curious French lavender, *Lavandula stoechas* 'Willow Vale'. Some years ago there was a fashion for borders of silver foliage plants. While silver

OPPOSITE: ***Cistus x argenteus* 'Silver Pink' is an excellent compact shrub for a hot, dry, sunny location, flowering profusely in early summer.**

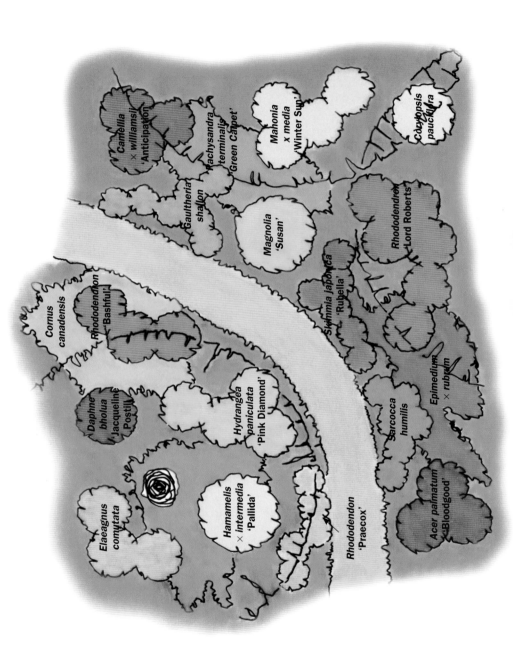

Camellia × williamsii 'Anticipation'

Pachysandra terminalis 'Green Carpet'

Gaultheria shallon

Mahonia x media 'Winter Sun'

Corylopsis pauciflora

Cornus canadensis

Rhododendron 'Bashful'

Magnolia 'Susan'

Skimmia japonica 'Rubella'

Rhododendron 'Lord Roberts'

Daphne bholua 'Jacqueline Postill'

Hydrangea paniculata 'Pink Diamond'

Sarcococca humilis

Epimedium × rubrum

Elaeagnus comutata

Hamamelis × intermedia 'Pallida'

Rhododendron 'Praecox'

Acer palmatum 'Bloodgood'

The plan for a shade border shows some of the possibilities of this type of planting. The soil has a low pH, allowing the use of acid-loving species such as rhododendron and camellia. Spring and early summer will be the peak flowering time for most of these choice plants. Many of the shrubs make quite large specimens so spacing is generous to allow them to grow and still be individually appreciated from the central path. Carpets of woodland groundcover link the groups together and the ideal accompaniment to all this would be a generous planting of spring bulbs, possibly followed by lilies for summer colour.

foliage makes an excellent contrast in a planting scheme and 'silvers' thrive in hot, dry conditions, they can be rather dreary on their own, so do mix them with the other foliage and flowers. Some also have interesting flowers of their own, such as *Perovskia* 'Blue Spire', *Caryoperis clandonensis* 'Kew Blue', *Hebe pinguifolia* 'Pagei' and the new *Buddleja* 'Silver Anniversary'. For an accent in such locations, probably the best selection would be a spiky *Yucca*, such as *Y. flaccida* 'Ivory', which will have a strong shape and eventually tall spires of white bell-shaped flowers.

Shrubs for shade

Gardeners often ask what to grow in a shady situation, whether this is the shade cast by a large building or underneath a tree. Although shade does provide a limiting factor, there are many plants, and particularly shrubs, which will not only survive in shade but actually prefer to grow and thrive in conditions of reduced sunshine. Take a visit to any good woodland garden such as the Savill Gardens or Wakehurst Place and you will find a whole host of exquisite and colourful shrubs that thrive in low light conditions.

When shade is also coupled with dry conditions, such as you would find underneath the dense canopy of mature trees, then the problem becomes a little bit more difficult. But there are still lots of plants that will survive in such conditions. Most of the evergreen *Euonymus*, hollies, the native *Hippophae rhamnoides*, most of the *Mahonias* (particularly *M. aquifolium*), *Osmanthus*, *Sambucus* and *Viburnum davidii* will grow in dry shade. All are good garden shrubs with good foliage and some with flowers and berries. When planting in such conditions, part of the problem may be that the soil under a mature tree is compacted and thick with existing roots. If you want new plants to establish, you will have to cultivate the surface and improve the soil with organic matter. You need to create a fresh rooting zone for your new plants without excessive competition from the existing tree. Watering in the first season, coupled with a good thick mulch, is essential.

Moist shady conditions are comparatively easy and many shrubs will revel in such conditions. *Camellia*, *Rhododendron*, *Skimmia*, *Hamamelis*, *Elaeagnus*, *Cornus* and *Hydrangea* all thrive in such an environment. The common mophead hydrangeas are too familiar to need description. There are also the more delicate lacecaps, the late-flowered *H. paniculata* with pointed panicles of white or pink flowers, *H. quercifolia*, mainly grown for its oak-like foliage, and *H. arborescens* 'Annabelle' with huge mopheads of white blossom.

Acid lovers

You might have admired rhododendrons or camellias growing in a public garden, have bought one and taken it home, only to have it sulk and for its leaves to turn a sickly yellow. This is because

This healthy plant of *Skimmia japonica* is showing spring flowers as well as last year's remaining berries.

some choice shrubs will only grow successfully in acid soils. Such soils will have a pH of less than 6.5, which often occurs in soils that have a high natural content of sand or peat. Plants which need an acid soil are also sometimes called calcifuge, meaning that they will not tolerate chalk or lime (calcium) in the soil, which raises the pH. They are sometimes called lime haters. Amongst this group of plants there are all the members of the family *Ericaceae*, which include the vast genus *Rhododendron*, heathers, blueberries and a few other related plants.

Then there is the genus *Camellia* and a number of other choice shrubs that like similar conditions and are well worth growing. Members of the genus *Pieris* are particularly known for the brilliant red young growth that cultivars such as 'Forest Flame' make in spring. Almost all of them will also produce showy panicles of small white or pink flowers. The common name 'Lily-of-the-valley shrub' describes the flower shape but they are not scented. *Kalmia latifiolia* is a lovely evergreen shrub that comes from California and produces large clusters of rich pink flowers in midsummer. There are a number of cultivars with either white or two-tone flowers. If you have the right conditions, do try growing *Crinodendron hookerianum*, a choice evergreen from Chile. It

is a large upright shrub with narrow dark green leaves and each summer produces clusters of small, deep crimson flowers like tiny lanterns.

Skimmias are often grown for their bright red winter berries. These particular plants are said to be dioecious, meaning that male and female flowers are on separate plants. Both are needed for pollination to take place and berries to be formed on the female plants. For example you might choose *Skimmia japonica* 'Veitchii' for its berries and *Skimmia japonica* 'Rubella' as the male pollinator. Fortunately, as well as being useful, 'Rubella' is very attractive, producing striking spires of bright red buds which over the winter months slowly open to scented pink flowers. One male *Skimmia* will pollinate about three females. The cultivars of *Gaultheria mucronata* (previously *Pernettya*) are similar plants in some ways, having vivid pink, red or white berries and also being dioecious. 'Mulberry Wine' produces a rich, almost purple, berry and 'Bell's Seedling' is a good deep pink and is also hermaphrodite, so does not require a pollinator. *Gaultheria shallon* is an excellent woodland ground cover plant that spreads by suckers. It has glossy green leaves and small white bell-shaped flowers tinged with pink that are followed by purple berries. It's a good colonizer for shady locations, as is *Leucothoe fontanesiana*.

A small woodland show garden featuring *Rhododendron* 'Roseum Elegans' with *Digitalis* 'Pam's Split' and other shade-loving species.

CREATING SHADE

Some gardeners may have the right soil conditions and want to try growing some of these choice shrubs but do not have the dappled shade. Quite simply – plant your own small spinney! Probably one of the easiest shade trees to grow is the birch. The native *Betula pendula* is cheap to purchase and fast-growing but rarely becomes a problem. There are also some lovely choice birches such as the white-stemmed *B*. 'Grayswood Ghost', the cut-leaved *B. pendula* 'Laciniata', or the abominably named but pretty *B. albo-sinensis* var *septentrionalis* with pink bark. All are relatively cheap, generally available and will quickly make some light shade. As soon as they become too large or the shade is too dense, thin the branches or remove some of the trees. You can even stool them, cutting them hard to ground level. Thin the resulting regrowth to three strong shoots and in time you will get an attractive multi-stem birch that will be a feature in its own right.

This slow-growing plant produces bottle-green leaves together with trailing racemes of small white flowers. The cultivar 'Rainbow' has leaves that are attractively variegated with reddish-pink, white and creamy-yellow. As you will see, a garden in the shade need never be drab and colourless, particularly if you have an acid soil!

Chalk-tolerant shrubs

Fortunately, a large number of familiar good garden shrubs will tolerate chalky soils with a high pH. In particular, *Osmanthus*, *Viburnum*, *Kolkwitzia*, *Buddleja*, *Hibiscus*, *Rosmarinus*, *Ligustrum*, *Philadelphus*, *Ceanothus*, *Chaenomeles*, *Pyracantha* and *Mahonia* are very tolerant. Really chalky soils will also tend to be shallow, stony and therefore drier. Good deep cultivation will help to increase the potential rooting zone, and generous dressings of organic matter will improve the water-holding capacity. Always mulch shrub plantings on shallow soils.

Waterlogged conditions

Most good gardeners will probably want to try and correct any waterlogged areas by improving drainage. However, there are some shrubs which will grow in the damp soil alongside a stream or

Sinocalycanthus × *raulstonii* 'Hartlage Wine' is a fairly new and unusual shrub that revels in shady moist conditions.

even in a problem wet patch. All the dogwoods, members of the genus *Cornus*, will tolerate wet, badly drained soils, as will the bushy willows such as *Salix* 'Britzensis'; both provide coloured winter stems. Planting such species will help to dry up a waterlogged site because they will absorb large quantities of water. *Sambucus* and *Physocarpus*, both grown for coloured foliage, as well as the various *Hydrangea*, *Philadelphus* and *Spiraea* are also tolerant of moist soils. *Parrotia persica*, grown for its autumn colour, needs a moist but well-drained site.

SHRUBS FOR DIFFERENT PURPOSES

Some shrubs are particularly useful in the garden because they fulfil a purpose. Climbers will hide an ugly oil tank or clothe a blank wall. Tough

This showy, large-leaved ivy is correctly known as *Hedera colchica* 'Sulphur Heart' but is sometimes sold as 'Paddy's Pride'.

shrubs can provide shelter from harsh winds and prickly shrubs will boost your home security. Then there are others which will encourage wildlife to your garden: birds, bees and butterflies. So as well as being attractive, many shrubs can fulfil basic functions in your garden.

Climbers and wall shrubs

Climbers are woody plants with a lax habit and the ability to attach themselves to a support. Wall shrubs, although similar, have no means of support but are shrubs that either need the protection of a wall or are loose-growing and look best when trained against a wall or trellis. Among them there are species suitable for almost any situation, from full sun through to dense shade. If you have a hot, dry, south-facing wall, you might choose to grow an *Abutilon vitifolium*, a native of South America, which will revel in the warmth and produce an early summer spectacle of pale blue saucer-shaped flowers. Then a cold north-facing wall would be ideal for *Jasminum nudiflorum*, with its succession of brave yellow winter flowers, or one of the many variegated ivies such as *Hedera helix* 'Goldheart' with its small green leaves adorned with a brassy golden splash.

Climbers grow and attach themselves in several different ways. The climbing hydrangea and all the ivies produce aerial roots that cling to rough surfaces such as stonework. These shrubs can be planted against a wall and left to grow on their own without any support. Unless the mortar between the bricks is actually loose and crumbling, they will not harm the building. However, you will need to be careful if they grow vigorously and reach the roof line, as they are inclined to creep under the tiles and invade your roof space. Also be aware that if you change your mind and decide to remove an old ivy, it will leave behind a matrix of tiny roots which will disfigure the wall until they disintegrate. Virginia creeper, *Parthenocissus tricuspidata* 'Veitchii', has tendrils with suckers on the end which help it to stick to blank walls. It also leaves a mess if removed. These climbers are sometimes called self-clinging as they do not need a support.

CLIMBERS FOR SUNNY WALLS

Vitis coignetiae AGM – vigorous ornamental vine, large green leaves, glowing autumn colour
Clematis montana 'Tetrarose' AGM – bronze-tinted leaves, large pink flowers in late spring
Wisteria sinensis AGM – vigorous, sweetly scented long trusses of lilac flowers, early summer
Fremontodendron californicum 'California Glory' AGM – large bright yellow flowers, summer
Campsis × *tagliabuana* 'Madame Galen' AGM – soft red flowers in large clusters, late summer

CLIMBERS FOR SHADY WALLS

Garrya elliptica 'James Roof' AGM – evergreen wall shrub, long silvery catkins in winter
Parthenocissus henryana AGM – dark green velvety foliage with silver veins, autumn tints
Jasminum nudiflorum AGM – winter jasmine, green shoots, tiny leaves, yellow flowers
Hydrangea petiolaris AGM – glossy pale green leaves, large heads, white lacecap-style flowers
Hedera colchica 'Sulphur Heart' AGM – evergreen, large glossy leaves with large gold splash

CLIMBERS FOR OBELISKS AND TRELLISES

Clematis viticella 'Etoile Violette' AGM – slender climber, purple flowers, cream centre, summer
Rosa 'Gertrude Jekyll' AGM – New English Rose, glowing pink, strong scent, compact climber
Trachelospermum jasminoides AGM – evergreen, glossy leaves, fragrant white flowers
Lonicera periclymenum 'Belgica' – early Dutch honeysuckle, scented cream and purple flowers
Jasminum officinale 'Fiona Sunrise' – golden foliage, scented white summer flowers, vigorous

Some climbers such as the hardy passion flower, *Passiflora caerulea*, have waving tendrils that will grab hold of anything nearby. *Clematis* have long flexible leaf stalks which can curl around twigs or small supports in a similar way. Honeysuckle and wisteria have twining stems which wind around a support or other plants. All of these are ideal for growing on trellises and up pergolas and obelisks. If you want these on brick or concrete walls you will need to provide a supporting trellis or alternatively a matrix of galvanized wires, fixed to the wall. Wires are a very useful way of supporting climbers: inconspicuous when first installed and rapidly disappearing as the climbers grow.

Wall shrubs include plants like *Solanum crispum* 'Glasnevin' and *Abutilon megapotanicum*, which are very lax in their habit of growth and will benefit from being trained against a support. Others such as the colourful-leaved *Actinidia*

This exciting double flowered clematis is called 'Crystal Fountain' and is a moderate grower in Group 2, so should be lightly pruned.

WIND-TOLERANT SHRUBS

Corylus maxima 'Purpurea' AGM – purple hazel nut, purple catkins, foliage and nuts
Hippophae rhamnoides – UK native, sea buckthorn, silvery foliage, orange berries
Viburnum opulus – snowball tree, round pom-poms of white flowers, early summer
Viburnum tinus – reliable evergreen, white flowers throughout winter
Berberis × *stenophylla* AGM - dense evergreen foliage, masses of yellow flowers, early summer
Ilex × *altaclerensis* 'Lawsoniana' AGM – spineless, evergreen gold foliage, red berries
Tamarix tetrandra – tamarisk, spreading shrub, tiny leaves, sprays of pink flowers, scent
Salix exigua – thickets of suckering stems, small silvery leaves, spring catkins

SALT-TOLERANT SHRUBS

Escallonia rubra var *macrantha* – evergreen, glossy foliage, rose-crimson flowers in summer
Pyracantha 'Mohave' – vigorous evergreen, orange-red berries, disease resistant
Sambucus racemosa 'Sutherland Gold' AGM – golden elder, delicate golden foliage, tough form
Spiraea 'Arguta' AGM – bridal wreath, dense stems, masses of tiny white flowers, summer
Olearia × *haastii* – daisy bush, evergreen, fragrant white flowers, midsummer

kolokmikta are slightly tender and will benefit from the warmth of a south- or west-facing wall. *Argyrocytisus battandierii* can be grown as a small tree but prefers the protection of a wall and will reward you with silvery foliage, lovely yellow blooms and a delicious pineapple scent. Although hardy, the classical fig *Ficus carica*, with its wonderful 'Greek statue-shaped' foliage, needs a warm wall if you hope to produce edible fruit. The evergreen *Magnolia grandiflora* is strong growing and doesn't need the support of a wall but benefits from the extra shelter, giving huge glossy green leaves and giant round, bowl-shaped blooms in creamy white.

Beware of east walls that seem to be warm because they receive early morning sunshine. Never use them for planting winter-flowering species such as *Camellia, Jasminum nudiflorum, Viburnum* × *bodnantense* or *Mahonias*. When winter flowers become frozen, they need to thaw slowly to avoid being damaged, but if they get early morning sunshine the plant cells are likely to be ruptured as ice crystals thaw (just like the burst pipe effect). Better to put winter-flowering species on west or north facing walls.

Shrubs for shelter

Some gardeners may find themselves with an exposed garden that is beaten by wind or particularly prone to frost. In this situation you will need to plant trees and shrubs for shelter. A living shelter belt is nearly always better than a fence or wall because it filters and slows the wind rather than causing turbulence. Ideally, plant a shelterbelt in advance and allow it to establish for a few years before you plant choice shrubs that may be damaged by the weather. In really exposed locations you may need to use a man-made windbreak fabric or woven wattle fencing to provide some initial protection.

Security gardening

Ask any crime prevention officer about landscaping and they will usually suggest cutting everything to ground level, which is rarely an acceptable option for most gardeners! If vandalism or the risk of burglary is an issue, consider planting some dense and prickly species to protect vulnerable areas. Almost any thorny plants will help but

Pyracantha 'Orange Glow' is a popular and reliable tall shrub producing copious quantities of colourful berries each autumn.

some are better than others. *Crataegus prunifolia* makes one of the densest and prickliest boundary hedges imaginable and it looks good, with rich autumn colours and bright red fruits. *Berberis gagnepainii* and *B. julianae* are both armed with long spines, and hollies have prickly leaves. The ornamental brambles such as *Rubus cockburnianus* and *R. ulmifolius* 'Bellidiflorus' both have long, arching spiny stems that make an impenetrable barrier. The unusual *Rosa sericea* subsp *omiensis* × *pteracantha* may be almost impossible to say but is easy to grow. It not only has small white flowers but is armed with huge translucent red thorns that look beautiful in summer and harden by winter to make a dense thicket. Any plants with dense twiggy growth will act as deterrents. Tall shrubs or hedges of species such as *Viburnum* or *Escallonia* are almost impossible to push through, and low shrubs with long trailing stems such as *Cotoneaster* and *Juniperus* make excellent trip hazards!

Climbers on buildings can either be a deterrent or an open opportunity to intruders. Never use heavy-duty squared trellis on a wall underneath an upstairs window. Instead, use tensioned vertical wires which are impossible to climb. If you have a climber such as *Wisteria* that makes stout climbable branches, consider adding a prickly rambler rose to train over the branches.

Shrubs for wildlife

Much emphasis has been placed on the use of native species in landscape schemes over recent years but this is often not appropriate in the private garden situation or even in commercial landscapes. Studies at Sheffield University have concluded that urban gardens, both large and small, planted with ornamental plants are very successful at encouraging and supporting wildlife. Gardens are amazingly diverse, even compared to

natural habitats, because they are so variable and, as such, excellent at supporting wildlife. In particular trees, hedges and shrubs are successful in providing valuable habitats. Lots of vegetation means many different places to live and a greater supply of food. The study goes on to say that untidy gardens where plants are allowed to go to seed and their fallen autumn leaves are left undisturbed provide ideal conditions. This does not necessarily tie in with some good horticultural practices but if attracting wildlife is important, then this is a good excuse not to tidy your garden!

Some plants will have particular characteristics that make them more attractive to wildlife as well as being ornamental. *Buddleja*, lavender, *Sambucus* and lilac are all excellent shrubs for attracting butterflies. Bees will be particularly drawn to *Ceanothus, Cytisus, Escallonia, Berberis, Hypericum, Fuchsia, Potentilla, Spiraea* and *Weigela*.

Most of the berried shrubs can provide winter food for birds but in particular *Cotoneaster, Pyracantha, Viburnum opulus, Ilex* and *Berberis* such as *B. darwinii* and *B. wilsoniae* are particularly suitable. Climbing honeysuckle and mature ivy will also produce berries which seem to be liked by certain birds. Of course many plants attract insects which in turn also act as a food source for birds. *Buddleja globosa* is said to be particularly good for this. Large shrubs and particularly thorny plants are also good for birds as they provide safe nesting sites.

Of course wildlife gardening is a composite process involving many different types of plants and trees as well as the shrubs we have described here. It also involves many other activities such as composting and the provision of other habitats such as ponds and meadows.

OPPOSITE: **There are many different cultivars of lavender, most of which produce scented blue flowers in midsummer that are popular with bees and butterflies.**

BELOW: **This flowering quince, *Chaenomeles speciosa* 'Simonii', is an excellent source of early nectar for bees.**

4 SOME CELEBRITY SHRUBS

Among the many thousands of shrubs in cultivation, there are a few genera that are both more extensive than others and have for various reasons caught the attention of plant lovers through the generations. Gardeners have faced the challenge of growing these difficult species; plant breeders have persevered with creating bigger, better and more perfect hybrids; and others have just swooned at the sheer beauty that these plants can provide. It would be difficult not to have fallen in love with at least a few of these shrubby celebrities!

FAVOURITE GENERA

Some plants are undoubtedly more popular than others and highlighted here are just three: *Rhododendron*, *Camellia* and *Rosa*. To give you some idea of their popularity and complexity, between them they have nearly 9,000 entries in the Plant Finder, which means 9,000 essentially different plants – quite a range!

Rhododendrons

This is probably one of the most opulent of all genera, much loved by Victorian gardeners who craved the new species brought home from China, Tibet and North America. Rhododendrons are a vast group of plants with over 1,000 species and 28,000 recorded cultivars. The first cultivated rhododendron was the pink-flowered *R. hirsutum*, introduced from Europe in 1656. Probably the most commonly known of all is the fast growing *R. ponticum*, with not unattractive lavender blue flowers. It is not a UK native, originating from southern Europe and southwest Asia, but has colonized many areas. It should be considered a pernicious weed, because it smothers most of the understory in woodlands and prevents regeneration of tree species. Many of the garden species and hybrid rhododendrons make large, impressive evergreen shrubs with showy trusses of flowers in various shades of pink, salmon, red, and lavender. Many are richly scented. The flowering season extends from early spring right through to early summer. In height they vary from tiny alpine shrubs through to specimens of many metres, more easily considered as trees.

There are now countless compact cultivars, more suitable for small gardens, and many of these have been bred from *R. yakushimanum* from Japan. As well as attractive flowers, they have small leaves with silvery hairs on the underside and when young the new growths are covered in a cinnamon coloured 'felt'. There are also some evergreen azaleas with small leaves and copious flowers. A few cultivars have variegated foliage, such as the somewhat gaudy 'President Roosevelt' with flowers of raspberry ripple colour and gold-splashed foliage. Despite their spectacular displays in early summer, most rhododendrons tend to be drab evergreens for the remaining eleven months of the year.

The classification of rhododendrons is complex and some are also commonly called azaleas. In particular there are many deciduous azaleas that have been bred from *R. luteum*, which is a yellow-flowered deciduous species with sweet scent and superb reddish autumn colour. You will hear of Ghent, Knaphill, Exbury and Mollis azaleas.

OPPOSITE: The huge genus of *Rhododendron* includes many rare types such as this spectacular hybrid between *R. protistum* × *R. grande*.

In the following tables, rhododendrons are classified by height as Small: 60–75cm (2ft–2ft 6in); Compact: 75cm–1.2m (2ft 6in–4ft); Medium: 1.2–2.1m (4ft–7ft); Tall: over 2.1m (7ft). Flowering seasons are divided into Mid Season: mid to late spring; and Late season: late spring to early summer.

In recent years, a range of rhododendrons have also been grafted on a patented revolutionary 'Inkarho' rootstock that is tolerant of lime. Results and opinions on this seem to be varied but it is said that these plants will grow on soils with a pH up to 7.0. If you have the wrong soil but want to grow rhododendrons, these are definitely worth trying.

Name	Colour	Season	Height
Hardy hybrid rhododendrons			
'Fastuosum Flore Pleno' AGM	Lavender blue, semi-double	Mid–late	Tall
'Purple Splendour' AGM	Purple with black edges	Mid–late	Tall
'Dreamland' AGM	Pale pink, edged deep pink	Mid–late	Compact
'Mrs Charles E. Pearson' AGM	Mauve buds, pink flowers, brown spots	Mid–late	Tall
'Lord Roberts' AGM	Dark crimson red	Mid–late	Medium
'Gomer Waterer' AGM	White flushed mauve pink	Mid–late	Medium
'Roseum Elegans'	Soft lavender pink	Mid–late	Tall
'Albert Schweitzer' AGM	Warm pink with brown centre	Mid–late	Tall
***R. yakushimanum* hybrids**			
'Bashful' AGM	Rose pink with reddish brown blotch	Mid–late	Compact
'Pink Cherub' AGM	Rose pink with pale centre	Mid	Compact
'Dopey' AGM	Deep glossy red	Mid–late	Compact
'Koichiro Wada' AGM	Pink buds opening to pure white	Mid	Small
'Golden Torch'	Peach buds, creamy yellow flowers	Mid–late	Small
'Hoppy'	Pale lilac fading to white	Mid	Compact
Evergreen azaleas			
'Blue Danube' AGM	Large blue-violet	Late	Medium
'Blaauw's Pink' AGM	Salmon pink, medium hose-in-hose flowers	Late	Medium
'Vuyk's Rosyred' AGM	Rose red with darker flash, large	Mid	Compact
'Niagara'	White with deep chartreuse blotch	Mid	Compact
Deciduous azaleas			
'Homebush' AGM	Deep carmine, paler shading, autumn tints	Mid	Med–tall
'Fireball' AGM	Orange red with dark flare, autumn tints	Mid–late	Medium
'Klondyke' AGM	Orange gold, tinted red, autumn colour	Mid–late	Medium
'Daviesii'	Cream opening to white	Late	Medium
'Anneke'	Lemon yellow, autumn tints	Mid	Medium
'Persil' AGM	White with orange yellow flare	Mid	Medium

Camellias

You will undoubtedly know of *Camellia sinensis*, although possibly not by its botanical name. This is the source of the beverage tea, made from its young leaves, and is an important commercial crop in China, India, Kenya and Sri Lanka. In addition there are over 3,000 species and named cultivars of *Camellia* grown for their flowers. These glossy-leaved evergreens originate from woodland areas, from the Himalayas through to China and Japan. They are much loved for their beautiful, often many-petalled flowers in whites, pinks and reds. Most flower in late winter and early spring and although the plants are generally hardy, flowers may be browned by spring frosts. Growing them in sheltered locations or under the cover of light woodland will give ideal conditions for producing an undamaged display.

Camellias such as this brave 'Freedom Bell' need to be sited away from morning sun to allow frozen blooms to thaw slowly.

The many species and cultivars are divided into six groups based on their flower shape. Many of the older camellias are cultivars of *C. japonica*, including old favourites such as the semi-double scarlet 'Adolphe Audusson' and the white-flowered 'Desire'. The showy flowers of 'Tricolor' are semi-double and streaked with pink, white and red. From 1940 onwards an increasing range of *Camellia* × *williamsii* hybrids have been introduced, including the delicate pink 'J.C. Williams', named after its raiser. These hybrids are generally tough and free-flowering. Possibly the most popular is the brilliant pink semi-double 'Donation', an exceedingly reliable and free-flowering cultivar.

A number of interesting cultivars have been developed from *Camellia sasanqua*, a small-leaved species from Japan. The hybrids tend to be more sun tolerant and useful as landscape plants. Many are autumn blooming and some have the added bonus of perfume.

Growing Rhododendrons and Camellias

Rhododendrons and camellias grow best in the dappled shade provided by light woodland. They prefer a well-drained, humus-rich and acidic soil. Rhododendrons grow best with a pH of 4.5–5.5, whilst camellias will tolerate pH5.5–6.5. If you do not have a naturally acidic soil, it is possible to modify soil conditions to some extent and lower the pH. Traditionally this was often done by using large quantities of peat but many gardeners would now find this environmentally unacceptable. Alternatively you can use flowers of sulphur or sulphur chips at a rate of $100g/m^2$ ($3ozs/yd^2$) for every unit drop in pH. For example, if you want to drop from pH7.5 to 5.5 you will need $200g/m^2$ ($6ozs/yd^2$). Sulphur may be available from garden stores or large pharmacies but the cheapest sources are likely to be found on the internet. Altering soil pH with sulphur is effective but will take at least a season to work, so it is preferable to apply it well in advance of planting. Couple this with generous dressing of organic matter to generally improve the soil structure. Alternatively, grow acid loving plants in pots using a proprietary acid compost.

Name	Form	Colour	Season	Height
Camellia japonica types				
'Elegans' AGM	Anemone	Rose pink	Early	Spreading
'Akashigata' (syn 'Lady Clare') AGM	Semi-double	Soft pink	Early-mid	Spreading
'Adolphe Audusson' AGM	Semi-double	Blood red	Mid	Compact
'Desire' AGM	Double	Ivory blush	Early-mid	Upright
'Lavinia Maggi' AGM	Double	Pink/white striped	Mid-late	Upright
Camellia × williamsii hybrids				
'Donation' AGM	Semi-double	Clear pink	Mid	Upright
'Anticipation' AGM	Peony	Rose cyclamen	Mid	Upright
'Ruby Wedding' AGM	Double	Red, white centre	Mid	Upright
'E.T.R. Carlyon' AGM	Semi-double	White	Early	Upright
Camellia sasanqua hybrids				
'Hugh Evans' AGM	Single	Rose pink	Autumn	Upright
'Jean May' AGM	Double	Shell pink	Autumn	Upright
'Sparkling Burgundy'	Anemone	Lavender pink	Autumn	Upright

Do not plant camellias or rhododendrons too deeply and keep well watered during dry weather, preferably with rainwater. This is particularly important during summer with camellias, to avoid bud drop which can entirely destroy the next year's flowering potential. Neither plant requires regular pruning, although both respond well to the removal of the dead flowers that prevent the plant's energy being directed to seed production. Old, leggy rhododendrons can be rejuvenated by pruning hard back to about 20cm (9in), although you need to be careful not to prune back beyond the union where the plant was originally grafted. If you do this in error you will unfortunately only get the regeneration of the rootstock, which is likely to be an old cultivar called 'Cunningham's White'. Camellias that get too big for their location can also be hard pruned. They will regenerate well but you will lose at least a season's flowering potential.

Shrub roses

Roses are a wonderful but massive specialist collection of plants that are often considered on their own. They are native to many parts of the world and have been widely hybridized, producing thousands of cultivars. However, one particular group, the shrub roses, fits neatly into the theme of this book. Shrub roses are quite a diverse group that includes the original wild species and some very old cultivars, most of which have a loose, open habit and make large shrub-like plants. They are divided into groups linked with the species they were bred from, so you will find hybrids of the old, many-petalled cabbage rose *R. centifolia*, such as 'Fantin Latour', a free-flowering double pale pink rose. Other groups include R × alba, *R × bourboniana*, *R. chinensis*, *R. damascena*, *R. gallica* and the hybrid musk roses. Sadly, although most of the older types are charming in many ways, they usually have a very vigorous

OPPOSITE: The Punchbowl in the Savill Gardens demonstrates the exuberant summer colour available from some of the azaleas.

Rhododendron 'Firelight' is a good compact hybrid, looking attractive here against the dark leaves of *Heuchera* 'Hollywood'.

habit, typically only flower once in the season, and may be prone to mildew and black spot.

However, there are many good shrub roses. Try *Rosa moyesii*, which has elegant lacy foliage and single red flowers followed by flagon-shaped hips. It makes a big plant and can be well over 2.5m (8ft) tall, although there is a more compact version called *R. m.* 'Geranium' (not to be confused with the genus *Geranium!*). Then there is *Rosa xanthina* 'Canary Bird', which makes a large bush clothed with arching sprays of small, yellow, scented single roses in early summer. Although it has only one display season each year, it is well worth growing. The lovely old 'William Lobb', introduced in 1855, has dark crimson, many-petalled flowers with silvery reverses. It is sometimes called a moss rose because of a moss-like appearance to the buds. There are also many modern shrub roses, such as 'Frülingsmorgen', which is perpetual flowering with pretty single pink flowers and maroon hips.

In particular, it is worth highlighting the roses of David Austin, who since 1969 has been breeding and growing a group of roses called the New English Roses. These are particularly good garden plants, having much of the charm of old roses, such as many petals and a strong scent, alongside excellent garden performance, repeat flowering and disease resistance. One of the best of these is the yellow 'Graham Thomas' but there are many others such as the rich ruby 'Darcey Bussell' and the clear pink 'Brother Cadfael'.

Shrub roses integrate well with other shrubs and with herbaceous perennials and bulbs in mixed plantings. Shrub roses are very easy to grow, requiring minimal pruning. Although they are tolerant, do not neglect them altogether. A spring feed coupled with a mulch of rotted farmyard manure or garden compost will encourage a good display on healthy plants. In particular, be careful not to dead-head them if you want the autumn display of hips, particularly important with the species roses and those that have a single flowering season.

Climbing and rambler roses are especially tall, lax cultivars that can be trained against all sorts of supports, trellises, archways or pillars. They do not attach themselves, so need tying in place. Climbing roses are trained to leave a semi-permanent framework of branches, and flowering side-shoots are pruned back to this framework each spring. Occasionally a main branch should be removed to ground level to stimulate new growth.

'American Pillar' is a rambler rose introduced in 1902 but still an excellent choice where vigour and an intense colour are needed.

FAVOURITE SHRUB ROSES

There are so many thousands of roses that a short list in a book such as this can barely touch the surface. Those listed are my own favourites!

'Graham Thomas' AGM – a lovely yellow New English Rose 1.5m (5ft)
'Nevada' AGM – older shrub rose, huge white single flowers 2.1m (7ft)
'Climbing Cécile Brünner' AGM – tiny but perfect fully double pink flowers 4m (13ft)
R. banksiae 'Lutea' AGM – climber, small double yellow flowers, prune lightly 6m (20ft)
R. filipes 'Kiftsgate' AGM – very vigorous rambler, masses of white flowers 10m (30ft)
'Climbing Étoile de Hollande' AGM – deep red climber, very strongly scented 4.6m (15ft)
'Scarlet Fire' AGM – large shrub rose, single red flowers and fine hips 3m (10ft)
R. sericea subsp *omiensis* f *pteracantha* – glowing red thorns, small white flowers 2.1m (7ft)

'Graham Thomas' is one of David Austin's New English Roses, seen here with a background of *Sambucus nigra* 'Black Beauty'.

Climbers include old favourites such as 'Étoile de Hollande' and 'Mermaid' as well as modern cultivars such as 'Compassion' and 'Golden Future'. Some of the more lax New English Roses, such as 'James Galway', 'Graham Thomas' and 'A Shropshire Lad', can be used as compact climbers for training on objects such as obelisks. Pruning will need to be lighter than if you were growing them as bushes.

By contrast, rambling roses produce long cane-like growths from ground level each year. These flower in the second year and then the old canes must be removed to encourage fresh growth. 'American Pillar', which is pink, and 'Wedding Day', a prolific white, are both good ramblers. One of the most vigorous and free-flowering is *Rosa filipes* 'Kiftsgate', which will make a gigantic plant covered in huge trusses of tiny white scented flowers with prominent yellow stamens. Use it to cover an ugly building or blank wall.

Rosa banksiae 'Lutea' is another unusual and very attractive climber which delivers an enchanting display of miniature double yellow flowers in late spring. It is the exception to most roses in that it flowers only on old wood, so pruning should only be very light just to keep it within bounds and remove a proportion of old wood each year.

Winter heathers, cultivars of *Erica carnea*, look cheerful from the first flowers in late autumn through to when they finally fade in late spring.

SUPPORTING CAST

As well as these prima donnas of the shrub world, there is a whole supporting cast of others, grouped together because of origin, botanical features, use or culture.

Heathers

Heathers belong to the same family as rhododendrons, although by comparison they are mostly quite diminutive plants, making dense carpets of tiny leaves topped with small spikes of colourful flowers. Botanically, heathers can be members of the genus *Erica*, *Calluna* or *Daboecia*, all part of the family *Ericaceae*. There are many species and cultivars of the genus *Erica*, such as the very welcome *E. carnea* cultivars that flower throughout the winter. These heathers are the exception in that they are lime tolerant and do not need an acid soil. 'Springwood White' is a traditional and reliable white, 'Pink Spangles' a soft pink and 'Myretoun Ruby' a good deep red. The closely related hybrids listed as *E. × darleyensis*, hybrids between *E. erigena* and *E. carnea* such as 'White Perfection' and the pink 'Darley Dale', also flower in the winter but tend to be slightly taller.

The summer flowering species need an acid soil and include cultivars of *E. cinerea*, *E. tetralix*, and *E. vagans*. As well as these, there are the many different types of *Calluna vulgaris*, which is of course the native ling. They tend to have a slightly more upright and open habit and narrow elongated spikes of flowers in late summer and early autumn. 'County Wicklow' is a good soft pink and 'Darkness' has rich crimson flowers. There are also some golden-leaved cultivars such as 'Beoley Gold'. The Irish heaths, members of the genus *Daboecia*, also flower in the summer.

There are also a few tree heaths, although they are really more shrub-like. The commonest of these is probably *E. arborea*, which is native to many countries including Europe, the Mediterranean and parts of Africa. It makes an upright bush with long spikes of honey-scented white flowers in the spring. The cultivar 'Alpina' is quite compact and grows to no more than 1.8m (6ft). *E. australis* is pink flowered but slightly tender so must be grown in a sheltered location.

All heathers like an open, sunny position and well-drained, humus-rich soil. During the early years after planting they will respond well to an annual dressing of a general fertilizer, followed by topping up any mulch. Both the winter and summer flowering heathers should be trimmed over with shears or hedge trimmers in mid to late spring. Rake off the trimmings and remove to avoid the development of disease. Tree heathers should have the flowering shoots lightly trimmed in late spring (see Chapter 9 for propagation).

JUST A FEW OF THE MANY HEATHERS

Name	Description	Season	Height
Erica carnea 'Springwood White' AGM	Spreading, white flowers	Winter	30cm (1ft)
Erica carnea 'Myretoun Ruby' AGM	Deep ruby red flowers	Winter	25cm (9in)
Erica carnea 'Pink Spangles' AGM	Soft pale pink flowers	Winter	25cm (9in)
Erica × darleyensis 'Darley Dale'	Shell pink flowers, spreading	Winter	60cm (2ft)
Erica × darleyensis 'Silberschmeltze'	Pure white	Winter	30cm (1ft)
Erica arborea var alpina AGM	Dense spikes of white flowers	Spring	1.5m (5ft)
Erica australis	Spikes purplish pink flowers	Spring	1.8m (6ft)
Erica vagans 'Lyonesse' AGM	Pure white flowers	Summer	25cm (9in)
Erica vagans 'Mrs D.F. Maxwell' AGM	Deep rose pink flowers	Summer	30cm (1ft)
Calluna vulgaris 'Darkness' AGM	Rich ruby red	Summer	25cm (9in)
Calluna vulgaris 'Beoley Gold' AGM	Golden foliage, white flowers	Summer	35cm (15in)
Calluna vulgaris 'Peter Sparkes' AGM	Double rose pink flowers	Summer	45cm (18in)
Daboecia 'William Buchanan' AGM	Deep crimson flowers	Summer	30cm (1ft)
Daboecia cantabrica alba	White flowers	Summer	25cm (9in)

Beautiful bamboos

These dramatic architectural plants are actually woody grasses and have the added benefit of being evergreen. Most are tall soaring plants, excellent as specimens and useful for the back of the border or for screening. The striking canes can be green, gold or black, sometimes with stripes or a bluish hue to them. *Phyllostachys nigra* is the so-called black bamboo and *Phyllostachys vivax* 'Aureocaulis' has vivid golden canes with green stripes. The latter has gently running roots but is not unduly invasive, although it can be quite disconcerting when a brilliant golden cane emerges in the middle of your lawn! *Fargesia murieliae* has elegant small green leaves and makes a tall screening plant. If you want variegated foliage, try the tongue twistingly named *X Hibanobambusa tranquillans* 'Shiro-shima' which has large glossy green leaves with creamy stripes and a moderate habit. *Pleioblastus auricomus* is also variegated with stripy golden foliage and makes excellent groundcover. This dwarf bamboo behaves rather more like a grass and you can cut it down to ground level each spring and allow it to regrow with a small forest of gilded foliage.

The blue bamboo, *Himalayacalamus hookerianus*, produces steely-blue new canes that mature to a rich orange.

Bamboos are rewarding plants but gardeners are scared to plant them because of their reputation for being invasive. Just be careful to check out the species before purchasing and select only those that are referred to as 'clump-forming'. Alternatively, you can construct a root barrier with really tough plastic to keep them within an allotted space.

Bamboos are not fussy and respond nicely to a well-prepared and rich garden soil, giving vigorous growth, well-coloured canes and lush green foliage. They can be successfully grown in large pots or tubs, using a good loam-based compost for stability. Once established, you can enhance the appearance of bamboos with coloured canes by carefully removing the leafy side shoots up to about 1.8m (6ft), which will reveal the striking coloured canes. Old or dying canes can be removed, generally thinning the clumps, but otherwise do not prune. Clumps of bamboo trimmed with hedge-trimmers or shears look awful!

A SELECTION OF BAMBOOS

Name	Description	Habit	Height
Phyllostachys nigra AGM	Shiny black stems, green foliage	Clumping	4m (13ft)
Phyllostachys vivax 'Aureocaulis' AGM	Vigorous, vivid golden-yellow canes with green stripes	Spreading	4m (13ft)
Fargesia murieliae	Green canes and small green leaves	Clumping	2.4m (8ft)
Chusquea culeou	Green foliage, graceful habit	Clumping	3.6m (12ft)
X Hibanobambusa tranquillans 'Shiroshima' AGM	Glossy green leaves with cream variegations	Active	2.1m (7ft)
Pleioblastus auricomus AGM	Compact, striped golden foliage	Active	1.5m (5ft)

For variegated foliage, *X Hibanobambusa tranquillans* 'Shiroshima' is probably the best tall hardy bamboo.

Conifers

This is a huge group of fascinating plants that have received negative coverage in recent years, particularly because of the bad habits of the Leyland cypress *X Cupressocyparis leylandii,* which is a large, fast-growing parkland tree that should never be planted in small gardens. Its inclusion in totally inappropriate places has led to unpleasant neighbourly disputes and even lawsuits. There are no bad plants, just bad places to plant them! Most of the big conifers are wonderful trees, many with important significance in the timber industry, but they must be planted in woodlands and parks where there is room for them to grow.

The shrubby conifers are much smaller evergreen plants, slower growing and often stylishly shaped, in various shades of green, gold and almost blue. Many have strong vertical outlines and as such make excellent statements in a planting scheme, whereas others have a prostrate habit and are valuable groundcover plants. *Chamaecyparis lawsoniana* 'Ellwoodii' makes a small dark green spire, slowly reaching 1.8m (6ft). It is often sold for rock gardens or as a small plant for winter window box display. Many of the junipers make low groundcover, such as *Juniperus × media* 'Gold Coast' with its gold tipped foliage and *J. virginiana* 'Grey Owl', which makes

Conifers are available in a whole range of greens, golds and silvery-blues, as this nursery display demonstrates.

SOME SHRUBBY CONIFERS

Name	Description	Habit	Height
Chamaecyparis lawsoniana 'Ellwoodii' AGM	Bluish-green feathery foliage	Upright, narrow	1.8m (6ft)
Juniperus x pfitzeriana 'Old Gold' AGM	Prickly, bright golden foliage	Spreading	90cm (3ft)
Juniperus 'Grey Owl' AGM	Fine soft-grey foliage	Prostrate	45cm (18in)
Juniperus squamata 'Blue Star' AGM	Prickly, intense steel-blue foliage	Bushy	30cm (1ft)
Thuya occidentalis 'Rheingold' AGM	Gold foliage turning coppery in winter	Upright, rounded	1.8m (6ft)
Pinus mugo 'Mops' AGM	Mountain pine. Needle-like green leaves, small cones	Rounded	90cm (3ft)

Hebe 'Midsummer Beauty' is a fairly hardy and vigorous cultivar that produces masses of midsummer flowers, loved by bees and butterflies.

an almost flat carpet of fine silvery-grey foliage. *Pinus mugo* var *pumilo*, the dwarf Swiss mountain pine, makes a compact bun shape with typical needle-like foliage and, once established, small pine cones.

In general, conifers do not need pruning. Occasionally, vertical conifers can tend to open up, sometimes as a result of snow damage. In this instance, the best treatment is to gently tie the plant back into shape using green garden wire wrapped around the foliage. Conifer hedges can be lightly trimmed with shears or a hedge trimmer to get a formal effect but should never be cut back into the old wood, as they will not regrow. Avoid removing the leading shoots from conifers as this will cause the growth of multiple new leaders and a very odd-shaped plant.

New Zealand shrubs

Among the many exciting garden plants from New Zealand, the *Hebes* are undoubtedly the most useful. This genus includes colourful flowering and foliage plants, with everything from compact little buns growing to no more than 15cm (6in) up to substantial bushes 1.8m (6ft) tall and as wide. The compact *Hebe pinguifolia* 'Pagei' makes a small mound of pewter-grey foliage, topped in early summer with clouds of white flowers. 'Carl Teschner' is another carpeting cultivar, this time with green leaves, black stems and pale blue flowers. At the other end of the scale, 'Great Orme' will make a 1.2m (4ft) bush covered in summer with bright pink flower spikes, fading to white; a great favourite with butterflies and bees. *Hebe franciscana* 'Variegata' has green leaves with broad cream margins and short, soft-purple flowers. It is often seen as a window box or container plant. There are also a few that have totally different leaves, called whipcord foliage, that are more like a conifer; 'James Stirling' is a golden version. In recent years numerous new cultivars have been released, including those with vivid multi-coloured leaves such as 'Heartbreaker'. If you have a sheltered spot, try the slightly tender 'La Seduisante', with large racemes of brilliant red flowers in late summer. All are readily available and worth growing.

Hebes are easy to grow but prefer a sunny, sheltered site and a well-drained soil. Their hardiness varies. As a generalization, the compact cultivars with small leaves are hardier than the large-leaved types with long flower spikes. Generally they require little attention and no pruning unless frost damages the top growth.

As well as *Hebes*, many other shrubs regularly grown in UK gardens have originated from New Zealand. There are spikey *Cordylines*, glossy-leaved *Griselinia*, *Olearia* and many different lacy-leaved *Pittosporums*, all grown for their attractive foliage. The basic *Pittosporum tenuifolium* is a good evergreen with small apple-green leaves, black stems and chocolate-coloured, honey-scented flowers. It makes a large shrub or small tree. The various coloured-leaved cultivars are more compact and less hardy. 'Irene Paterson' has white speckled leaves and 'Garnettii' bold white margins with pink splashes. Both need a sheltered location. There are several gold-leaved cultivars such as 'Tandara Gold' with its tiny leaves. The cultivar 'Tom Thumb' is very short, slowly reaching about 1.2m (4ft) in height and being one of the very few evergreen shrubs with true purple foliage. The Plant Finder lists sixty-six different cultivars so there is plenty of choice.

The name *Cordyline australis* causes confusion as this plant originates from New Zealand. *Cordyline* is a genus of many-hued evergreen spiky plants, sometimes called cabbage palms, although there is no relationship to real palms. You may see tree-size specimens of the plain green *C. australis* or the bronze-leaved 'Purpurea'. Eventually these will produce white flowers but the strong sweet perfume can be almost overpowering in close proximity! As well as these reliable traditional types, there are some wonderful coloured types such as 'Black Tower', with lustrous dark foliage, the white variegated 'Torbay Dazzler', or 'Sundance' with its red leaves suffused with green. Look out for 'Pink Stripe', a recent cultivar with vivid ruby and rich pink foliage.

The *Griselinias* are another group of handsome evergreen shrubs. The plain glossy-green *G. littoralis* makes a valuable background or screen-

Despite originating from New Zealand, *Griselinia littoralis* 'Dixon's Cream' is amazingly tough and hardy.

ing plant and is salt tolerant for maritime areas, but is easily upstaged by the variegated types for garden display. Look out for the cultivars 'Dixon's Cream' or 'Bantry Bay', both with glossy leaves generously splashed with glowing gold.

Most gardeners know the sprawling silver-leaved, yellow-flowered daisy bush, now *Brachyglottis* but known for many years as *Senecio*. *B. monroi* is a more compact version of this with neatly crimped leaves, and there is also a new introduction, 'Silver Dormouse'.

Members of the genus *Corokia* have pretty little yellow flowers and the cultivar 'Sunsplash' has prettily variegated leaves. *Coprosmas* are inclined to be tender but have wonderful polished leaves in different colours. Both make compact bushes.

Garden centres often promote *Sophora microphylla* 'Sun King', an evergreen wall shrub with delicate pinnate leaves and drooping yellow fuchsia-like flowers. Then there is *Clianthus puniceus*, another showy New Zealand wall shrub. The dark

green pinnate leaves show off the rich coral-red flowers, like lobster claws, produced in summer. Both need a well-drained, sheltered wall, facing south or west, and grow to about 1.8m (6ft) in height.

Now from the sublime to the ridiculous: *Pseudopanax ferox* is a plant to grow for its curiosity value rather than its beauty! Its common name of toothed lancewood describes the hanging juvenile foliage, which is serrated like a double-sided freezer knife. It usually grows as a single stem with its armoury of bronze leaves hanging down like a bizarre Christmas tree. It is never really attractive but certainly an eye-catcher and talking point for those who like unusual plants. It is virtually hardy, given a sheltered spot and good drainage.

Tender shrubs

There are many gardeners who like the challenge of growing plants on the borderline of hardiness. Some gardeners develop this into the style often called exotic gardening, which aims to create a jungle-like appearance using both hardy and tender plants. Such gardening can be very rewarding, seeing plants from warm countries thriving in a chilly climate!

Plants with dramatic leaves are always eye-catchers and amongst these one of the most exciting is *Tetrapanax papyrifer*, a native of Taiwan. It can in time make an impressive shrub as much as 3m (10ft) in height, dressed with huge, deeply cut palmate leaves. Severe winters may cause this

Site *Tetrapanax papyrifer* in a sheltered location to encourage vigorous growth and huge, dramatic leaves.

With its long flowering season, *Grevillea* 'Canberra Gem' from New Zealand is well worth a sunny spot in the garden.

plant to die back to ground level, but don't despair as it will usually sucker from the root stock and quickly form an acceptable plant once again. There are a number of species of *Schefflera* that also have dramatic foliage. *S. taiwaniana* and *S. delavayii* are both worth growing for their showy foliage and may well prove hardy in many areas. *Melianthus major* is a subshrub from South Africa with finely-cut silver foliage. In mild winters it will retain its woody structure and then may reward you with scented deep red flowers in late summer. In hard winters it will die to the ground but usually suckers again from the roots.

Most abutilons originate from South America and are either tender or borderline hardy. The beautiful blue *Abutilon vitifolium* and its white counterpart 'Tennant's White' both have huge saucer-shaped flowers. There are also a number of smaller-flowered species such as the diminutive *A. megapotanicum* with baggy, petticoated flowers in yellow and maroon with black paintbrush stamens. All need a sheltered wall to give winter protection and encourage them to flower in early summer.

Callistemon, from Australia, is known for its showy red bottlebrush flowers in early summer. Both *C. rigidus* and *C. citrinus* 'Splendens' are almost hardy but should be given a sheltered location in the full sun. You may also like to try *C. pallidus*, which has pale lemon-yellow flowers, or some of the newer cultivars in shades of pink. The genus *Grevillea* is also native to Australia and a number of species and cultivars are well worth trying in a temperate climate. The cultivar 'Canberra Gem' produces an airy, feathery shrub covered in needle-like foliage, similar to a feathery rosemary bush. In spring and early summer it will produce a succession of clusters of spidery pink flowers. There are others such as *G. juniperina × sulphurea* which has yellow flowers. Give them a well-drained location in full sun and they will flower copiously for weeks. There are many different species of *Acacia* from Australia, most of which are too tender for the UK. However it is worth trying *A. dealbata* or *A. baileyana*, both of which will make large shrubs covered with very delicate silvery-green foliage and masses of lemon-yellow flowers. Most people would recognize this as the florist's mimosa.

The angel's trumpets originate from South America, so most are too tender and require greenhouse protection. Most produce huge fragrant flowers. *Brugmansia sanguinea* is the toughest of them all, growing naturally at high altitudes in its native Andes. It is worth trying against a warm wall, where it should produce a succession of rich orange and yellow trumpets and, with a

little protection, may survive most winters. There are many others worth gambling with, such as *Erythrina crista-gali* from South America, *Nerium oleander* from the Mediterranean, or *Euphorbia mellifera* from Madeira.

Most plants of borderline hardiness will require a little extra attention to guarantee their success. Good drainage is essential, so make sure the ground for tender plants is thoroughly cultivated and, to be sure, add some extra grit or sharp sand. Ideally, plant tender shrubs against a south- or west-facing wall, to receive the maximum sunshine. Brick walls are ideal as they retain some of the day's warmth at night. Tender plants will appreciate a little extra protection during the winter, especially during their initial years after planting. Create a small structure using three to five bamboo canes or small stakes and stretch horticultural fleece or sacking around. You can also pack the centre with loose straw. Be sure also to give such plants a good thick mulch of loose organic matter, such as leaf mould or bark. This will insulate the roots from winter cold. With all of these horticultural gambles, success may not be permanent. Such plants may grow and thrive for say five years but then succumb to a hard winter in the sixth. That is not failure, when you consider the five years of pleasure they have given you!

In mild areas where frost is rare, *Brugmansia aurea* provides a spectacular display of scented trumpet flowers.

Rogue's gallery

Amongst all the many wonderful shrubs, there are a few that for various reasons should be avoided! One of the worst is *Sasa veitchii*. The edges of the coarse green leaves die back, leaving brown margins, said by some to be attractive. As well as its unendearing appearance, it spreads rapidly and is almost impossible to eradicate. *Rhododendron ponticum* is far too coarse and invasive, so never plant it. Check out buddlejas carefully. Some older cultivars set seed regularly and unless you remove all the old flower spikes, seedling buddlejas can be a distinct weed problem. *Buddleja globosa* is a large coarse shrub that always seems to be dirty and dusty! Hypericums can be very prone to rust disease, particularly the pretty cultivar 'Elstead'. *Polygonum baldschuanicum* is sometimes recommended as a vigorous climber, which it certainly is. Eventually reaching 12m (40ft) or more, it really is too much of a monster for most locations. Avoid the unimproved versions of most shrubs such as laurel, weigela, forsythia and so on. They may well crop up, poorly labelled, amongst bargain batches of shrubs. Most will be extremely vigorous and have limited flower power. There are so many excellent shrubs that there's no reason for planting these rogues!

***Sasa veitchii* might be described as one of the 'thugs' of the shrub world and should rarely be planted due to its invasive nature.**

5 THIRTY NEW AND WONDERFUL SHRUBS

New plants are the lifeblood of commercial horticulture, avidly promoted by the garden centre industry and hungrily snapped up by curious gardeners. Sometimes new shrubs are chance occurrences, seedlings or mutations. Other plants are the result of painstaking hybridization over many years, with many failures before the achievement of success.

The story behind *Choisya* 'Sundance' is a tale of both chance and skilled plantsmanship. Peter Catt, a British nurseryman, noticed a small leaf with a white edge on a plant of the green-leaved *Choisya ternata*. The shoot with this leaf was rooted as a cutting and surprisingly, when grown on, it eventually produced shoots with golden leaves. It was launched as a novelty at the Chelsea Flower Show in 1986. So from the acute observation of one small leaf that was different came an award-winning plant that grows in so many gardens today. Since then there has been a regular flow of Peter's introductions in a whole range of genera including *Spiraea*, *Potentilla* and *Caryopteris*.

By contrast, other introductions are the result of deliberate breeding programmes and years of careful selection and trialling. However, there are relatively few people actively involved in hybridizing shrubs. One such person is Peter Moore, propagator at Longstock Gardens and previously at Hilliers, although his hybridization work is a hobby and much of the work is done in his own garden. His first major success was also a *Choisya*, the cultivar 'Aztec Pearl' introduced in 1989.

Then for ten years he worked with this, crossing it with 'Sundance' before he produced the one gold seedling that became 'Goldfingers', first marketed in 2000.

Peter Moore looks after the National Collection of *Buddleja* at Longstock and has been responsible for a number of new *Buddleja* introductions such as 'Sugar Plum' and 'Silver Anniversary'. While some hybridizers work in a random way, allowing the bees to carry out pollination, Peter prefers to carry out hand pollination, keeping precise records of his crosses. Among Peter's other successes you will find *Cotinus* 'Dusky Maiden', *Spiraea* 'Sparkling Champagne', and *Weigela* 'Ruby Anniversary'. Others are on their way from the many crosses made over the last 30 years of painstaking work.

THE SHRUBS

Any selection of shrubs from the many thousands on offer has to be subjective. There are undoubtedly other good new shrubs that I haven't mentioned. I have also included a few older but outstanding plants, personal favourite shrubs – the privilege of being the author!

You may wonder why so few of them have an AGM, the prestigious award from the Royal Horticultural Society. Quite simply, most of these plants have not been in cultivation long enough for the trial and award system to be complete. However, most of these plants should be available from nurseries that list them in the Plant Finder or in good garden centres. Where there is a similar cultivar, this is also listed. In this chapter you will see the selling names in capitals and the registered cultivar names following – just to be correct!

OPPOSITE: **Flower shows, such as the annual Chelsea Flower Show, are the best places to see the best and newest plants at their peak in one location.**

Abelia × *grandiflora* 'Kaleidoscope'

A compact bush covered in variegated bright gold and green foliage, contrasting well with the thin red stems. A succession of white flowers throughout summer followed by good reddish autumn tints. In mild locations it may be evergreen. Fragrant flowers attractive to bees and butterflies.

Season of display Early summer to early autumn

Origin Hybridized by R. Lindsey and introduced in 2006

Height and spread 90cm × 1.5m (3ft × 5ft)

Aspect Full sun to light shade, best foliage colours in sun

Soil Prefers moist well-drained acidic soil

Propagation Softwood tip cuttings; licence required for commercial production

Cultivation Easy to grow, makes a good container plant

Pruning Generally not needed, except occasionally to shorten odd leggy shoots

Hardiness Totally hardy, Zone 6

Pests and diseases No particular problems

Availability Plant Finder: 21 suppliers; garden centres supplied by Bransford Webb

Similar plant *Abelia* × *grandiflora* 'Sunrise'

Associates with *Phormium tenax* 'Rainbow Maiden' – vivid orange-red strap-like foliage; *Cotinus coggygria* 'Atropurpurea' – bronze foliage, tall background plant; *Coreopsis verticillata* 'Moonbeam' – yellow daisy-like flowers, low herbaceous perennial; *Lilium* 'Montezuma' – deep red oriental lily, flowers midsummer

Berberis thunbergii 'Orange Rocket'

Small, strikingly shaped impact shrub. Vibrant coral-orange foliage, ageing to mid-green on narrow upright plant with columnar habit.

Season of display Late spring to autumn

Origin Selected by Michal Andrusiv in Litomysl in the Czech Republic, in 1994; hybrid from cross between *Berberis thunbergii* 'Aurea' and *B. t.* 'Helmond Pillar'

Height and spread 1.2m × 30cm (4ft × 12in)

Aspect Best foliage colour in bright sunshine

Soil Ordinary garden soil, drought tolerant when established

Propagation Softwood cuttings in summer; licence required for commercial production

Cultivation Easy to grow

Pruning None required except for occasional shaping

Hardiness Totally hardy, Zone 4

Pests and diseases Certified rust resistant

Availability Plant Finder: six suppliers; garden centres supplied by Bransford Webb

Similar plants *Berberis thunbergii* 'Golden Rocket', 'Golden Torch' and 'Helmond Pillar'

Brachyglottis Walberton's SILVER DORMOUSE ('Walbrach')

Attractive improved version of the familiar old shrub that was often called *Senecio greyii* or *S.* 'Sunshine'. This new cultivar has furry silver foliage and a dense compact habit. Free-flowering with masses of single yellow daisy flowers.

Season of display Evergreen, so foliage for twelve months plus flowers throughout summer

Origin David Tristan of Walberton Nursery in West Sussex; it was selected as a mutant growing among a batch of tissue cultured plants in 1996

Height and spread 90cm × 1.2m (3ft × 4ft)

Aspect Full sun

Soil Any well-drained soil

Propagation Semi-ripe tip cuttings; licence needed for commercial production

Cultivation Easy to grow

Pruning Generally not needed

Hardiness Generally hardy, Zone 8

Pests and diseases No particular problems

Availability Plant Finder: four suppliers; garden centres supplied by New Place Nurseries

Buddleja SILVER ANNIVERSARY ('Morning Mist')

Wonderful new butterfly bush, producing long panicles of creamy-white sterile flowers with an orange eye and sweet perfume. Show-stopping silver foliage. Does not set seed, so long flowering display and no unwanted seedlings. Like all *Buddlejas*, attracts bees and butterflies.

Season of display Late summer through to autumn

Origin Raised by Peter Moore, hybrid of *Buddleja crispa × B. loricata* 1998

Height and spread 1.5m × 1.2m (5ft × 4ft), nicely rounded habit

Aspect Full sun

Soil Good well-drained rich loamy soil but not fussy; drought tolerant when established

Cultivation Easy to grow, feed generously

Pruning Hard prune in late spring

Hardiness Totally hardy, Zone 7

Propagation Softwood tip cuttings in summer or hardwood cuttings in winter; licence required for commercial production

Pests and diseases Generally trouble-free

Availability Plant Finder: twenty-six suppliers; garden centres supplied by New Place Nurseries

Associates with *Sambucus nigra* 'Black Lace' – Almost black finely cut foliage, tall so use as a background; *Eupatorium purpureum* – Bold late summer perennial with rich claret-coloured flowerheads; *Heuchera* 'Berry Smoothie' – Low growing foliage perennial with raspberry-pink leaves; *Pennisetum setaceum* 'Rubra' – Tender summer grass, rich purple foliage, smoky-pink flowers

Buddleja x weyeriana 'Pink Pagoda'

Tall late-flowering shrub for back of the border. This very new plant has long shapely trusses of lavender-pink flowers, each with an orange eye. It does not set seed.

Season of display Late summer to early autumn

Origin Bred by Peter Moore, a hybrid of *B. × weyeriana × B.* 'Pink Delight', 1998

Height and spread 1.5m × 1.2m (5ft × 4ft)

Aspect Sunny location

Soil Well-drained fertile soil

Propagation Softwood tip cuttings or hardwood cuttings; licence pending

Cultivation Easy to grow, feed generously

Pruning Prune hard, late spring

Hardiness Totally hardy, Zone 7

Pests and diseases No particular problems

Availability Very new so look out for it in garden centres and at specialist plant fairs

Caryopteris × clandonensis STERLING SILVER ('Lissilv')

Compact flowering and foliage shrub. Silvery foliage that acts as a perfect foil for the bright blue flowers.

Season of display Deciduous so foliage from early summer and flowers from mid to late summer

Origin Raised by Peter Catt; seedling from *C. × clandonensis* 'Longwood Blue'

Height and spread Tidy compact habit, 90cm × 45cm (3ft × 18in)

Aspect Full sun

Soil Any fertile well-drained soil, drought resistant when established

Propagation Softwood tip cuttings; commercial production needs licence

Cultivation Easy to grow

Pruning Hard prune in mid-spring

Hardiness Generally hardy, Zone 8

Pests and diseases No particular problems

Availability Plant Finder: three suppliers; garden centres supplied by New Place Nurseries

Similar plant *Caryopteris × clandonensis* HINT OF GOLD ('Lisaura') – gold foliage

Ceanothus thyrsiflorus EL DORADO ('Perado')

Large, vigorous, upright-growing shrub with attractive limey-green variegated foliage and intense blue flowers.

Season of display Flowers late spring through early summer, evergreen so foliage for 12 months

Origin Sport of *C. thyrsiflorus* discovered in 1996 at Pershore College of Horticulture

Height and spread 2.4m × 2.4m (8ft × 8ft)

Aspect Full sun or light shade

Soil Ordinary well-drained garden soil, drought tolerant when established

Propagation Semi-ripe tip cuttings, late summer or early autumn; commercial production under licence

Cultivation Easy to grow, fast grower

Pruning Only prune if essential for containment

Hardiness Generally hardy, Zone 8

Pests and diseases No particular problems

Availability Plant Finder: three suppliers; garden centres

Similar plant *Ceanothus* 'Lemon and Lime', also 'Pershore Zanzibar'

Associates with *Hebe* 'Midsummer Beauty' – medium-sized shrub, pale blue flower spikes; *Phormium tenax* 'Yellow Wave' – spiky foliage plant with long golden-yellow leaves; *Caryopteris clandonensis* 'Heavenly Blue' – low growing, powder-blue flowers in late summer; *Geranium* 'Johnson's Blue' – herbaceous perennial, pale blue flowers in early summer

Ceanothus 'Tuxedo'

The first black-leaved ceanothus. Dark chocolate-coloured foliage all year round, plus lavender-blue flowers on tall shrub.

Season of display Evergreen, so foliage twelve months and flowers in late summer and autumn

Origin Sport from *C.* 'Autumnal Blue' raised by Fitzgerald Nurseries, Kilkenny, Ireland, appearing in 1998

Height and spread 1.8m × 1.8m (6ft × 6ft)

Aspect Needs bright sunlight

Soil Any well-drained soil; drought tolerant when established

Propagation Semi-ripe tip cuttings; commercial production under licence

Cultivation Easy to grow

Pruning Not essential but responds well to pruning

Hardiness Generally hardy, Zone 8

Pests and diseases No particular problems

Availability Plant Finder: five suppliers; garden centres supplied by Fitzgerald Nurseries

Choisya GOLDFINGERS ('Limo')

A golden-leaved version of 'Aztec Pearl' with narrow-fingered leaves. Bonus of delicate white scented flowers.

Season of display Evergreen, so twelve months of foliage interest plus flowers in early summer

Origin Result of a ten-year breeding programme by Peter Moore; hybrid between *C.* 'Sundance' and *C. dumosa* var *arizonica*, raised in 1994 and introduced in 2000

Height and spread 1.5m × 1.8m (5ft × 6ft)

Aspect Prefers full sun

Soil Any good well-drained soil

Propagation Semi-ripe tip cuttings in autumn; commercial production needs licence

Cultivation Easy to grow

Pruning None needed except for occasional shaping

Hardiness Generally hardy, Zone 8

Pests and diseases No particular problems

Availability Plant Finder: twenty-nine suppliers; garden centres

Cistus × *hybridus* LITTLE MISS SUNSHINE ('Dunnecis')

A small shrub with both foliage and flower. Delicate arrowhead-shaped leaves in gold and soft lime cover a compact plant, with the bonus of white saucer-shaped blooms with a pronounced orange centre.

Season of display Evergreen, so foliage interest for twelve months and flowers in early to mid summer

Origin Arose as a sport on mother stock at L & K Dunne Nurseries in Naas, Kildare, 2007

Height and spread 90cm × 90cm (3ft × 3ft)

Aspect Needs sheltered, warm, sunny location

Soil Well-drained garden soil, preferably sandy

Propagation Softwood or semi-ripe tip cuttings in summer and autumn; licence needed for commercial production

Cultivation Easy to grow, drought resistant

Pruning None needed

Hardiness Generally hardy, Zone 8

Pests and diseases No particular problems

Availability Plant Finder: two suppliers; garden centres supplied by New Place Nurseries

Associates with *Phormium tenax* 'Bronze Baby' – short New Zealand Flax with glossy coppery-red leaves; *Ceanothus* 'Blue Mound' – compact rounded evergreen with early summer blue flowers; *Crocosmia* 'Solfatare' – golden yellow flowers, light bronze foliage; *Alchemilla mollis* – frothy pale lemon flowers in early summer

Coprosma repens 'Tequila Sunrise'

Excellent patio plant with highly glossed, jewel-like foliage in brilliant shades of gold, orange, green, purple and red. Flowers are inconspicuous.

Season of display Evergreen, so twelve months colour

Origin Discovered as sport from *Coprosma* 'Yuanne' in New Zealand

Height and spread 90cm × 90cm (3ft × 3ft)

Aspect Partial to full sun, sheltered location

Soil Well-drained soil

Propagation Semi-ripe tip cuttings, commercial production requires a licence

Cultivation Easy to grow, needs some winter protection

Pruning Occasional shaping

Hardiness Borderline hardy, Zone 9

Pests and diseases No particular problems

Availability Garden centres

Similar plant *Coprosma* Pacific Sunset ('Jwn-copps')

Cornus VENUS ('Kn30 8')

Dramatic flowering dogwood with huge pure white bracts and green centres. Bracts may be as much as 20cm (8in) across and last two to three weeks. Bright autumn tints. Good as a specimen shrub.

Season of display Flowers in early summer plus autumn colour

Origin Hybrid between *Cornus kousa* var *chinensis* and *Cornus nutallii*; Dr Elwin Orton from the Rutgers University of New Jersey, USA, released 2003

Height and spread Vigorous – eventually makes a bush up to 5m × 5m (16ft × 16ft)

Aspect Full sun or partial shade

Soil Prefers mildly acidic soil, pH 6.1 to 6.5

Propagation Layering for small quantities, grafting; licence needed for commercial production

Cultivation Easy to grow; mulch well and feed

Pruning Occasional shaping only; prune after flowering to give maximum time for flower buds to form for next year

Hardiness Totally hardy, Zone 4

Pests and diseases Resistant to anthracnose and powdery mildew

Availability Plant Finder: eight suppliers; garden centres

Similar plants *Cornus* 'Eddie's White Wonder' AGM and 'Porlock' AGM

Cotinus coggygria GOLDEN SPIRIT ('Ancot')

Mainly a foliage shrub with leaves that start lime green and mature to rich gold, eventually turning brilliant orange and red before dropping in autumn. Traditional pinkish smokebush flowers. 'Best New Plant Introduction' at the 1999 Plantarium (Boskoop, Holland).

Season of display Deciduous, so foliage from late spring to autumn

Origin Selection by Adriana Sanders-van Harn from the Dutch nursery of Willem A. Sanders

Height and spread 2.1m × 1.8m (7ft × 6ft)

Aspect Full sun for best colourings

Soil Any good garden soil

Propagation Layering or softwood cuttings; licence needed for commercial propagation

Cultivation Easy to grow, makes a good container plant

Pruning Not essential but can be pruned to restrict size

Hardiness Totally hardy, Zone 4

Pests and diseases No particular problems

Availability Plant Finder: forty suppliers; garden centres

Associates with *Sambucus nigra* 'Black Lace' – tall shrub with finely cut black foliage; *Lavandula × intermedia* 'Grosso' – highly floriferous blue lavender; *Phormium tenax* 'Platt's Black' – compact New Zealand flax with almost black leaves; *Euphorbia wulfenii* 'Lambrook Gold' – bushy habit, silvery foliage and yellow bracts

Fothergilla × intermedia 'Blue Shadow'

Compact version of this classic plant, sweet honey-scented white bottlebrush flowers in spring. Summer foliage is steel blue, turning in autumn to brilliant orange and red.

Season of display Spring flowers, steely foliage throughout summer and autumn colour
Origin Sport from 'Mount Airy'
Height and spread 1.8m × 1.5m (6ft × 5ft)
Aspect Prefers partial shade
Soil Prefers moist, slightly acid soil
Propagation Softwood tip cuttings or layer; licence needed for commercial propagation
Cultivation Easy to grow
Pruning None needed except for occasional shaping
Hardiness Totally hardy, Zone 4
Pests and diseases No particular problems
Availability Plant Finder: nine suppliers; garden centres

Hebe 'Heartbreaker'

Compact foliage shrub for front of the border or as a patio plant. Produces a dwarf mound of white variegated foliage which assumes vivid pink tints during the winter. Occasional small mauve flowers in summer.

Season of display All the year round but best colours in winter; flowers throughout the summer
Origin A sport of 'Dazzler' discovered in the Netherlands
Height and spread 75cm × 75cm (2ft6in × 2ft6in)
Aspect Prefers full sun and sheltered location
Soil Well-drained but otherwise not fussy
Propagation Semi-ripe tip cuttings in early autumn; licence required for commercial production
Cultivation Easy to grow
Hardiness Borderline hardy, Zone 9
Pests and diseases No particular problems
Availability Plant Finder: sixteen suppliers; garden centres supplied by Lowater Nurseries
Similar plants *Hebe* PURPLE SHAMROCK ('Neprock'), 'Magic Summer' or 'Wild Romance'

Hydrangea macrophylla 'Zorro'

Good shade-tolerant shrub. Vivid blue-flowered lacecap hydrangea with distinct almost black stems.

Season of display Mid to late summer flowering

Origin Discovered by André van Zoest, on his nursery in Reeuwijk, Netherlands, as a naturally occurring mutation from 'Balumeise'

Height and spread 1.2m x 1.5m (4ft × 5ft)

Aspect Partial shade

Soil Fertile moist rich acidic soil

Propagation Softwood tip cuttings in summer; licence needed for commercial production

Cultivation Easy to grow

Pruning Cut back last year's flower heads in late spring, down to new flower buds

Hardiness Totally hardy, Zone 7

Pests and diseases No particular problems, may show chlorosis on alkaline soils and lose blue colouring

Availability Plant Finder: eleven suppliers; generally in garden centres from early summer

Associates with *Sambucus nigra* 'Black Lace' – tall background shrubs with lacy black foliage; *Ilex argentea* 'Marginata' – evergreen with white variegated holly leaves; *Hosta sieboldiana* var *elegans* – herbaceous perennial with large glaucous leaves; *Lilium regale* – lily with tall stately stems of white flowers

Jasminum officinale FIONA SUNRISE ('Frojas')

Vigorous climber with bright golden foliage that does not burn in sunshine. Bonus of scented white flowers throughout the summer, followed by black berries.

Season of display Foliage spring to autumn, flowers mid to late summer

Origin Discovered at Fromefield Nursery in the UK in 1989 in a batch of seedlings

Height 3m (10ft)

Aspect Full sun to partial shade

Soil Most good garden soils

Propagation Leaf bud cuttings in summer or layering; licence for commercial production

Cultivation Easy to grow; needs a trellis or other support to climb on; grows well through shrubs or mingled with other climbers

Pruning As necessary for containment

Hardiness Totally hardy, Zone 7

Pests and diseases No particular problems

Availability Plant Finder: forty suppliers; garden centres

Leycesteria formosa GOLDEN LANTERNS ('Notbruce')

This is the golden-leaved form of pheasant berry. Rich golden foliage, tinted with bronze when young. In midsummer it produces trailing spikes of flowers consisting of tiny white blossoms encased in reddish-purple bracts. Red-purple berries follow. Flowers attract bees and butterflies and fruit attracts birds.

Season of display Foliage from early summer and flowers from mid to late summer

Origin Bred by Notcutts Nurseries

Height and spread 1.5m × 1.2m (5ft × 4ft)

Aspect Needs full sun to get best leaf colour

Soil Flourishes on most soil types

Propagation Softwood cuttings in summer; commercial production under licence

Cultivation Easy to grow; mulch root system

Pruning Prune out weak stems in late winter

Hardiness Generally hardy, Zone 8 (root hardy to Zone 6 if mulched)

Pests and diseases No particular problems

Availability Plant Finder: twenty-eight suppliers; garden centres

Lonicera periclymenum 'Scentsation'

Deciduous climbing honeysuckle with bright creamy-yellow flowers and wonderful scent. Repeat flowering and red berries in autumn.

Season of display Mainly spring and early summer but through to autumn

Origin Found in a Herefordshire hedgerow by John Edmund and Els Wilms, who were attracted by its scent; introduced to the market by Bransford Webbs

Height 3m (10ft)

Aspect Sun or semi-shade

Soil Well-drained but moist soil

Propagation Layering or leaf bud cuttings

Cultivation Easy to grow; twining climber so needs a support such as trellis to grow on

Hardiness Totally hardy, Zone 7

Pests and diseases No particular problems

Availability Plant Finder: thirteen suppliers; garden centres supplied by Bransford Webb

Photinia × *fraseri* 'Little Red Robin'

Dwarf version of the popular evergreen shrub, grown for its glossy dark green summer foliage and particularly the vivid new growths that emerge bright scarlet. It has a bonus of snowy white flowers if left unpruned. Makes a good compact hedge.

Season of display Evergreen foliage twelve months, coloured new growths in spring and flowers in late spring

Origin Not known but likely to be a sport from the taller 'Red Robin'

Height and spread 90cm × 90cm (3ft × 3ft)

Aspect Prefers sunny location

Soil Any good garden soil

Propagation Semi-ripe tip cuttings in autumn

Cultivation Easy to grow

Pruning Rarely needed but will make a low hedge and can be trimmed

Hardiness Totally hardy, Zone 7

Pests and diseases No particular problems

Availability Plant Finder: twenty-four suppliers; garden centres supplied by New Place Nurseries

Physocarpus opulifolius DIABLE D'OR syn COPPERTINA in USA ('Mindia')

A compact deciduous foliage shrub, mainly grown for rich bronze foliage that has tints of gold when young. Clusters of tiny white flowers opening from red buds and followed by shiny red fruits. Similar to older 'Diabolo' but much more compact. Common name of Nine Bark because of splitting, flaking bark that is an added attraction.

Season of display Late spring through until autumn

Origin Raised in France, hybrid between 'Dart's Gold' and 'Diabolo'

Height and spread 1.5m × 1.5m (5ft × 5ft)

Aspect Prefers full sun

Soil Any good garden soil

Propagation Softwood tip cuttings in summer; licence required for commercial production

Cultivation Easy to grow

Pruning Can be pruned as hard as you like if just foliage required but if you want flowers just thin out some old growths after flowering

Hardiness Totally Hardy, Zone 6

Pests and diseases No particular problems, but being *Rosaceae* watch out for fireblight

Availability Plant Finder: thirteen suppliers; garden centres

Similar plant *Physocarpus* 'Lady in Red'

Associates with *Berberis thunbergii* 'Bonanza Gold' – shrub with small bright yellow leaves; *Potentilla fruticosa* 'Goldfinger' – low growing shrub with a succession of bright yellow flowers; *Crocosmia* 'Lucifer' – narrow green leaves and spikes of bright scarlet flowers; *Cistus* × *corbariensis* – compact shrub with masses of white flowers

Pieris japonica 'Katsura'

Valuable shade-loving evergreen. Delicate soft pink lily-of-the-valley style flowers in large clusters. Compact habit and glossy evergreen foliage with eye-catching ruby red new growths.

Season of display New growths in mid spring, flowers in late spring and early summer; year-round evergreen

Origin A sport from *Pieris japonica*, found on a wooded hillside near a Shinto Temple in Japan in 1986

Height and spread 1.2m × 1.2m (4ft × 4ft)

Aspect Partial shade

Soil Needs acid soil, fertile and well-drained

Propagation Semi-ripe cuttings in autumn; licence needed for commercial production

Cultivation Easy to grow, mulch and remove dead flower heads

Pruning Slow growing, no pruning needed

Hardiness Totally hardy, Zone 6

Pests and diseases No particular problems

Availability Plant Finder: thirty suppliers; garden centres supplied by New Place Nurseries

Similar plant *Pieris japonica* 'Passion'

Associates with *Camellia* × *williamsii* 'Inspiration' – evergreen, deep pink spring flowers; *Magnolia* 'Susan' – deep cerise-pink tulip-shaped flowers in late spring; *Tulip* 'Queen of the Night' – rich, almost black tulip; *Heuchera* 'Sparkling Burgundy' – herbaceous groundcover with crinkly wine-red leaves

Potentilla fruticosa 'Setting Sun'

Good reliable summer flowering shrub for front of the border. Compact habit with dense grey-green foliage and a succession of cheerful peach-coloured flowers.

Season of display All summer

Origin Raised by Alan Bremner in the Orkneys in 1989 as a result of open pollination of a selection of potentillas, but not registered until 2008

Height and spread 45cm × 30cm (18in × 1ft)

Aspect Full sun or partial shade

Soil Any good garden soil

Propagation Softwood cuttings in summer; licence needed for commercial propagation

Cultivation Easy to grow

Pruning None needed

Hardiness Totally hardy, Zone 3

Pests and diseases No particular problems

Availability Mainly garden centres supplied by Bransford Webb

Similar plant *Potentilla fruticosa* MANGO TANGO ('Uman')

Pyracantha SAPHYR ORANGE 'Cadange' AGM

Compact version of firethorn with dark green leaves, white flowers and brilliant orange berries. Berries attract birds. Thorny, so a good vandal and burglar deterrent. Can be grown as an informal hedge.

Season of display Evergreen, early summer flowers and autumn berries

Origin Introduced from France

Height and spread 1.5m × 1.5m (5ft × 5ft)

Aspect Partial shade or full sun; will tolerate north walls or exposed situations

Soil Prefers good soil but tolerates poor soils

Propagation Semi-ripe tip cuttings in autumn; commercial production requires licence

Cultivation Easy to grow either as a border shrub or trained against a wall; low maintenance

Pruning Occasional trimming for containment only

Hardiness Totally hardy, Zone 7

Pests and diseases The Saphyr range are resistant to both the fireblight and scab that affect many pyracanthas

Availability Plant Finder: twenty-three suppliers; garden centres

Similar plant *Pyracantha* SAPHYR RED ('Cadrou') and SAPHYR YELLOW ('Cadaune')

Rubus cockburnianus GOLDENVALE ('Wyego') AGM

Winter interest shrub, grown for its chalky-white winter stems and delicate, lacy golden foliage in summer. Arching prickly stems useful as vandal and burglar deterrent. Small purplish flowers and inedible blackberry-like fruits.

Season of display Summer foliage and winter stem colour

Origin Not known

Height and spread 2.1m × 2.1m (7ft × 7ft)

Aspect Grows well in dappled shade to avoid scorching the golden foliage

Soil Any good garden soil

Propagation Softwood tip cuttings or tip layers

Cultivation Easy to grow

Pruning Ideally prune hard to ground level each spring or alternatively every two years

Hardiness Totally hardy, Zone 6

Pests and diseases No particular problems

Availability Plant Finder: twenty-eight suppliers; garden centres

Associates with *Elaeagnus × ebbingei* 'Limelight' – vigorous evergreen with bright golden variegated leaves; *Cornus alba* 'Sibirica' – autumn colour and sealing-wax red stems in winter; *Euphorbia amygdaloides* var *robbiae* – evergreen groundcover with lime flowers in spring; *Bergenia* 'Evening Glow' – groundcover plant with huge leathery leaves that go bronze in winter

Sambucus nigra BLACK LACE ('Eva')

Stunning black-leaved shrub with finely cut foliage. Giant trusses of soft pink flowers in spring followed by black elderberries. Good for bees, butterflies and birds.

Season of display Deciduous, so summer foliage; early summer flowers and autumn berries
Origin Hybridized by Tobutt and registered in 2005
Height and spread 1.8m × 1.8m (6ft × 6ft)
Aspect Full sun for darkest foliage colour
Soil Any good garden soil but tolerates damp location
Propagation Softwood tip cuttings or hardwood cuttings; licence required for commercial production
Cultivation Easy to grow
Pruning Mainly for containment and shape; can be hard pruned to get just vigorous foliage but flowers will be sacrificed
Hardiness Totally hardy, Zone 4
Pests and diseases No particular problems
Availability Widely available

Santolina rosmarinifolia 'Lemon Fizz'

Golden-leaved version of the traditional cotton lavender with feathery chartreuse-coloured foliage. Soft yellow flowerheads in summer if left unpruned.

Season of display Evergreen, so twelve months but looks best in summer
Origin Not known
Height and spread 45cm × 45cm (18in × 18in)
Aspect Needs full sun
Soil Any well-drained soil; drought tolerant
Propagation Semi-ripe cuttings in autumn
Cultivation Easy to grow
Pruning Prune hard in mid spring almost back to ground level to stimulate vigorous foliage growth
Hardiness Generally hardy, Zone 8
Pests and diseases No particular problems
Availability Plant Finder: seventeen suppliers; garden centres supplied by New Place Nurseries

Spiraea 'Sparkling Champagne'

Compact shrub with foliage that emerges reddish purple to yellow in spring, fades to lime-green in summer and then turns glowing red and yellow before leaf drop. Lacy clusters of flower buds open to large flattened flowerheads of tiny flowers, each with pinkish-white petals and red stamens.

Season of display Main flowering in early summer followed by a later and smaller crop of flowers in late summer; autumn tints

Origin Raised by Peter Moore, *S. hayatana* × *S. japonica* 'Goldflame' 1998

Height and spread 75cm × 75cm (2ft6in × 2ft6in)

Aspect Full sun to partial shade

Soil Any good garden soil

Propagation Softwood tip cuttings; licence pending for commercial production

Cultivation Easy to grow

Pruning Not really needed but can thin out some older flowered shoots immediately after early summer flowering

Hardiness Totally hardy, Zone 6

Pests and diseases No particular problems

Availability Released 2010, likely to be available in garden centres soon

Associates with *Pittosporum tenuifolium* 'Garnettii' – evergreen, delicate white variegated foliage; *Weigela florida* 'Wine and Roses' – compact shrub, dark ruby foliage and deep pink flowers; *Penstemon* 'Andenken an Friedrich Hahn' (syn 'Garnet') – herbaceous, spikes of wine-red trumpets; *Artemisia* 'Powis Castle' – shrub, low cushions of filigree silver foliage

Weigela florida MONET ('Verweig')

Low-growing shrub, ideal for borders and patio pots. Stunning variegated foliage in subtle shades of green, pink and white from spring to autumn. Dark pink flowers.

Season of display Deciduous, so foliage interest throughout the summer to autumn; flowers in early summer

Origin Introduced in 2002 by Bert Verhoef, a renowned Dutch plant breeder

Height and spread 70cm × 90cm (2ft6in × 3ft)

Aspect Sun or semi-shade

Soil Well-drained soil

Propagation Softwood tip cuttings, early summer; licence required for commercial production

Cultivation Easy to grow and low maintenance

Pruning Just for shaping

Hardiness Totally hardy, Zone 6

Pests and diseases No particular problems

Availability Plant Finder: thirty-five suppliers; garden centres supplied by Bransford Webb

Yucca gloriosa BRIGHT STAR ('Walbrista')

A golden-leaved form of *Yucca gloriosa* which comes from south eastern USA. Dramatic rosettes of sharp-pointed, narrow, blue-grey leaves with a broad gold margin and pink tints. Young leaves produced vertically, maturing to a more horizontal position, giving a perfect hedgehog effect. Eventually flowers with an impressive spike of pink buds opening to white flowers.

Season of display Foliage for twelve months and flowers in mid to late summer

Origin Discovered by nurseryman Tim Crowther in 2000, whilst propagating offsets from *Y. gloriosa* 'Variegata', a paler-coloured leaf form

Height and spread Foliage 90cm × 90cm (3ft × 3ft) and flowers to 1.8m (6ft)

Aspect Full sun

Soil Well-drained, preferably light sandy soil

Propagation Offsets produced after flowering or toe cuttings; licence required for commercial production; most commercial stocks produced by tissue culture

Cultivation Easy to grow; drought-tolerant

Pruning Never prune except to remove dead flower spike after flowering

Hardiness Totally hardy, Zone 7

Pests and diseases No particular problems

Availability Notcutts garden centres and others supplied by John Wood Nurseries

Similar plant *Yucca gloriosa* 'Variegata'

6 DESIGNING WITH SHRUBS

As you will have seen, the world of shrubs is an amazingly diverse group of plants. Shrubs have foliage and flower in every colour imaginable, combined with perfume, berries, stem colour and a host of other interesting features. Shrubs come in every size, from flat little cushions that sit on the ground through to towering bushes many metres in height, and in every shape from soft graceful waterfalls through to spiky hedgehogs. So although designing only with shrubs to create a planting scheme might seem restrictive, there is an amazing palette of shrubs from which you can choose.

PUTTING SHRUBS TOGETHER

Planting schemes are often based primarily on shrubs, because they are such easy and accommodating plants. Shrubs are long-lived, require relatively little maintenance, do not need dividing every few years, are resistant to vandalism and generally tolerant of poor conditions and abuse. For this reason they are often used in commercial landscaping and for local authority work. However, even if the palette is limited to shrubs only, no planting scheme need ever be boring or unattractive. The following chapter will concentrate on designing with shrubs, although where appropriate will refer also to trees and plant associations with herbaceous perennials and bulbs.

OPPOSITE: **This small garden makes full use of a wide range of plants including trees, shrubs and herbaceous perennials, all beautifully integrated together.**

Designing with plants is a creative art form. However, we are dealing with living plants which grow and change with time and that makes it even more challenging. Shrubs, like all plants, have a number of characteristics, the most basic being colour, texture and form. Colour is self-explanatory but does of course encompass the colour of leaves, berries and stems as well as flowers, all of which alter with the seasons. Texture and form were introduced in Chapter 2 but need further explanation.

Texture and form

Texture refers to the pattern made by a plant's leaves or flowers. This can be most easily explained by comparing the tiny green leaves on a box plant with the huge chunky leaves on a bush of common laurel. The box produces a very delicate, fine texture, which is very different to the broad smooth surfaces of the laurel leaf. Fine textures have little difference between the surfaces that catch the light and the shadows behind, but with big leaves the differences between light and shade are dramatic, which gives large-leaved plants their punch. Some leaves may be large but still have a fine texture; *Aralia elata*, for example, has leaves that can be over 45cm (18in) long but are comprised of dozens of tiny little leaflets.

Form is all about the shape of a plant, sometimes called structure, which can be rounded, upright and narrow, low and spreading like a cushion, spiky or trailing. Plants with particularly striking shapes or outlines are often described as architectural plants. They can be especially useful as specimens, set in key locations in a planting scheme or positioned on their own as highlights in a lawn or paved surface. *Cornus controversa* 'Variegata' is a good example, with layers of horizontal branches decorated with delicately variegated small leaves. In early summer it also bears white flowers and in the autumn the foliage turns vivid pink before dropping. *Viburnum tomentosum* 'Mariessii' has a similar habit of growth, bearing layers of white flowers in early summer and good autumn colour. Other plants may have a spiky outline, such as the many types of *Yucca*. Bamboos will also come into this category, having a very dominant vertical shape, appealing canes and foliage. Contrasting different shapes together is one way of adding interest to a planting scheme. The upright habit of a clump of black bamboo, *Phyllostachys nigra*, could be contrasted with a low spreading carpet of *Juniperus media* 'Gold Coast'.

In some cases gardeners force a particular form onto a plant by the way it is pruned or trimmed, which is often called topiary. Both yew and box are available in a whole range of shapes, from cubes and balls through to pyramids, cones or spirals. Cloud trees are also very fashionable, consisting of a number of different-sized globes of tight clipped foliage on individual stems, all attached to the same plant. The small-leaved Japanese holly, *Ilex crenata* is often used to grow these. They tend to be very expensive but you can train your own. Such fancy shapes can provide exciting highlights in a planting scheme.

Building a planting scheme

When designing a planting scheme, one of the most important things to remember is that you are working in several dimensions, including time. It is sometimes difficult, when working on a sheet of paper, to imagine what plants will be like when they have reached their final stature in a few years. The more you can find out about a shrub's performance, height, spread, colour, seasons and so on, the better you will be equipped to design a successful scheme. Start off by marking in key plants such as trees and specimen shrubs that will act as the highlights within your border. Plants are usually simply drawn on a plan as scaled circles, roughly corresponding to their predicted mature diameter. You can use small circles of paper marked with the name of your chosen plants which can be juggled around until you get the desired result. There may be any number of key plants, but often three, five or seven are useful. So, for example, you might include a tree such as *Betula albosinensis* 'Pink Champagne', a birch with a delicate pink bark, a variegated evergreen such as *Pittosporum tenuifolium* 'Garnettii', and a spiky-leaved plant such as *Cordyline australis* 'Atropurpurea'. Position these in a triangular group, never in a row, in a way that marks the basic extent of the border. Specimen plants such

In this award-winning private garden, full use has been made of evergreens, autumn colour, conifers and clipped specimens.

as these are essential to emphasize the shape of the border; they act like exclamation marks.

Follow this by creating a matrix of strongly structural plants throughout the area. A high proportion of these should probably be evergreens, although good strong-growing roses and shapely deciduous shrubs can also be used. In choosing these plants, be aware of the backgrounds you are creating for the specimens you have already positioned. So you might plant a group of the variegated *Ilex aquifolium* 'Silver van Tol' around the dark-leaved *Cordyline* for the strongly contrasting foliage, and a dark-leaved *Corylus maxima* 'Purpurea' next to that. Add in *Sambucus nigra* 'Black Lace' next to the variegated *Pittosporum* and a rounded bush of *Ceanothus* 'Blue Mound' which again gives strongly contrasting foliage, flower and a mix of evergreen and deciduous. At

this stage you have really created the skeleton of your border, on which you can then build the detail with smaller shrubs, roses and herbaceous perennials. Tall plants do not always need to be positioned at the back of a border or the middle of an island bed. Plant some taller, well-shaped plants towards the front to give extra punch.

Design techniques

As you compose a planting scheme, you will always be trying to consider colour, texture and form as you put plants together to create stunning groups. Although a planting scheme for a border or even a whole garden may have an overall colour scheme and style, it is usually made up of a number of smaller components that are called plant associations. Putting together the black-

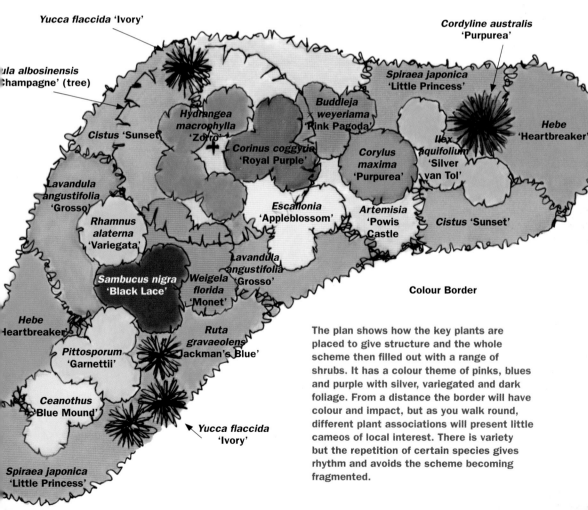

Colour Border

The plan shows how the key plants are placed to give structure and the whole scheme then filled out with a range of shrubs. It has a colour theme of pinks, blues and purple with silver, variegated and dark foliage. From a distance the border will have colour and impact, but as you walk round, different plant associations will present little cameos of local interest. There is variety but the repetition of certain species gives rhythm and avoids the scheme becoming fragmented.

leaved *Sambucus* 'Black Lace' with the silvery foliage of *Rhamnus alaterna* 'Variegata' and the blue
flowers of *Lavandula* 'Grosso' will give a lovely
cameo group: three different heights, some
contrasting colours and an interesting mix of
textures, using just three species. As you continue
to fill out your border, try to use groups of plants
that make good associations rather than just a mix
of your favourite plants. However, if you are careful you can both create good plant associations
and have your favourite plants.

Large specimen shrubs can be positioned as
individuals so that they stand out as special. With
most other plants, try to plant in groups of three,
five, seven and so on, as this will be most effective.
In a large border it helps if you repeat some of
the plants or groups at intervals down the border

On its own, this *Elaeagnus* 'Quicksilver' would be
unassuming, but in association with the vivid-
coloured rhododendron it looks quite striking.

or garden. In the plan shown, the blue lavender,
the *Hebe* and the pink *Cistus* are repeated. This
gives cohesion and is sometimes called rhythm.
Although variety creates interest, gardeners are
often tempted to use too many different plants, so
repeating a choice plant throughout the scheme
gives a unifying element. Such attention to detail
is the way to achieve a spectacular display.

Layering is another valuable planting technique in all gardens, but especially when space is
restricted. So underneath your birch tree, there
might be a group of three or five *Cotinus coggygria*
'Royal Purple', for its rich ruby foliage, contrasting agreeably with the pale pink bark of the birch.
Beneath this, plant some *Artemisia* 'Powis Castle'
to add a carpet of delicate silver foliage. Three
levels of interest, united to create a little cameo
of colour.

Shrubs come in every size imaginable, and
with many vigorous species there are also modern
compact or dwarf hybrids. So if you have a large
space to fill, by all means choose *Ceanothus*
'Trewithen', *Cotoneaster* 'Cornubia' or *Genista
aetnensis*, all tall vigorous shrubs. Just three plants
will soon make a huge block of foliage and flower.
But equally, in a small garden you could achieve
a similar effect with *Ceanothus* 'Blue Mound,
Cotoneaster horizontalis and *Genista lydia*, none of
which grow taller or wider than 90cm (3ft).

Beds and borders will come in all shapes and
sizes. In a small garden, they can sometimes be
too narrow to be really useful. Ideally, for a good
progression from front to back and to allow
contrasting heights and shapes, borders should be
at least 1.8m (6ft) wide. In many private garden
situations this will not be so. A border with a
width of 90cm (3ft) or less will only really accommodate one row of shrubs with some groundcover plants, so the opportunities immediately
become limited. Many of the taller shrubs will be
as wide as they are tall, so using anything with
height will immediately mean that the planting
juts out into the rest of the garden. In narrow
borders, wall shrubs and climbers become very
useful because you can have height and impact
without too much encroachment. Occasionally
you may have to contend with borders as narrow

as 30cm (1ft). Climbers and a few low-growing groundcover plants are really the only options, but with the range of climbers available even this need not be tedious.

Colour schemes

Although the primary emphasis in a planting design should be on good form and texture, the use of colour is also very important. Some people suggest that all colours go together in a garden but this is usually an excuse for poor design. In truth, mixed colours do not clash quite as much in the garden as they do indoors: the blue of sky, green of foliage and brown of soil tend to soften jangling colours. However, mixed colours tend to produce a riotous but rarely successful end result. Choosing two or three colours for a planting scheme is far more likely to achieve a winning result. In the previous sample plan, for example, the theme uses pinks and blues together with bronze and silver foliage.

Colour preferences are another very individual expression of our personality. Just look at the clothes people wear! Some of you will love hot colours: bright oranges, reds and yellows. Others will crave a cooler and more restful mix of blues, pastel shades, grey and silver. Both are totally acceptable. Sometimes a whole garden can be in a colour scheme, such as the famous white garden at Sissinghurst Castle; but it is more likely that you will choose a colour scheme for a border or a small part of a garden. Using just one colour can be dreary and monotonous, so although you might choose red as your key colour, you could add white flowers and bronze foliage. You could use *Chaenomeles* 'Knaphill Scarlet', *Cytisus* 'Killiney Red', *Photinia fraseri* 'Red Robin', *Escallonia* 'Red Elf' and *Rosa moyesii* 'Geranium', then add *Cotinus coggygria* 'Royal Purple' and *Cordyline australis* 'Purpurea' for bronze foliage, plus white flowers from *Cistus* × *corbariensis* and *Hydrangea paniculata*, and you will have an exciting balance of colours and interest.

Some colour schemes will use strongly contrasting colours such as orange and blue or yellow and purple; others will be gentler, with complementary colours that are close to each other such as blue and lavender or yellow and apricot. Pastel shades are colours with less intensity, such as pink, pale blue or cream, and most of these can be used together.

Avoid too much coloured or variegated foliage in a planting scheme, particularly with dominant plants such as specimens and trees. That golden-leaved *Elaeagnus pungens* 'Maculata' may

The 'Golden Lights' azalea contrasts well with the purple foliage of the *Acer palmatum* 'Atropurpurea' and the silvery-blue *Abies*.

have looked pretty in a garden centre but shrieks when mature and dominating your garden. Dark colours such as rich bronze foliage, deep maroon and midnight blues can be very attractive in catalogues but disappointing in the garden, particularly in shade. However, if you can position plants so that the sun shines through ruby-red foliage or dark chocolatey flowers, the effect can be quite dramatic. Whatever the colours chosen, you can freely use white, silver and also bronze foliage, all of which go with almost anything.

Planting styles

Shrubs can of course be arranged in many different ways. You could give the same plants to two landscape designers and they would probably create two totally different arrangements for you. The scheme described above is very much a basic shrub border, with a colour scheme and emphasis on summer interest. If you add herbaceous perennials, roses and maybe bulbs and bedding plants, it would be called a mixed border. Such plantings are rich with colour and interest throughout the year and would be successful in many garden situations. You may, however, be more ambitious and choose to arrange plants in any number of ways or themes.

Modern architecture demands a somewhat stylized and minimalist approach. A more restricted palette of plants would be used, probably with large sweeping masses of one plant, maybe a low ground cover plant such as *Euonymus fortunei* 'Dart's Blanket' that makes a dark green carpet. Injected into this might be a few carefully chosen specimen plants such as *Cornus controversa* 'Variegata', *Viburnum plicatum* × *tomentosum* 'Mariessii' or a bamboo such as *Phyllostachys aurea*. Other blocks of a different plant might be added such as *Skimmia japonica* 'Rubella', *Mahonia aquifolium* 'Apollo' or *Potentilla fruticosa* 'Goldfinger'. All are strong-growing shrubs that will make tightly defined blocks of foliage and flower. The aim is to use plants as blocks of colour and texture to complement the architecture. Nothing light and fluffy!

Borders can be themed for certain times of the

The tiny golden flowers of *Santolina virens* tone perfectly with the centres of the *Cistus* × *corbariensis*, flowering at the same time.

year, perhaps a special occasion such as an annual family party. An autumn border might include *Pyracantha* 'Orange Glow', *Cotoneaster* 'Rothschildianus' and *Rosa glauca*, together with *Parrotia persica*, *Euonymus europaeus* 'Red Cascade' and *Hamamelis mollis* for a fiery mix of berries and autumn colour. You might also want a scented border that could be filled with *Philadelphus*, *Syringa*, *Lavandula*, *Daphne*, *Mahonia*, *Sarcococca* and *Choisya*.

A woodland garden would aim to look very natural and informal. Plants would be in loose groups with lots of variety and different heights. Obviously the choice of plants would need to favour shade lovers. You could try *Camellia* 'Anticipation', *Hydrangea paniculata* 'Pink Diamond', *Rhododendron praecox*, *Magnolia* 'Susan' and *Corylopsis pauciflora*, all of which

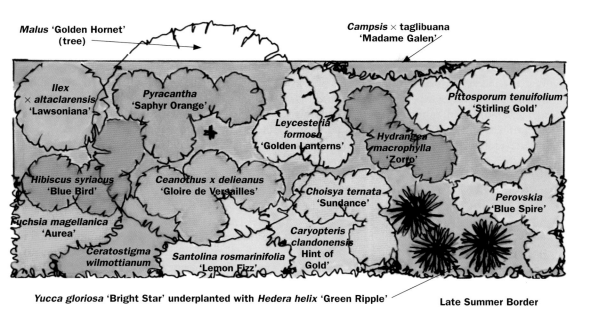

Malus 'Golden Hornet'
(tree)

Campsis × taglibuana
'Madame Galen'

Ilex
× altaclarensis
'Lawsoniana'

Pyracantha
'Saphyr Orange'

Pittosporum tenuifolium
'Stirling Gold'

Leycesteria
formosa
'Golden Lanterns'

Hydrangea
macrophylla
'Zorto'

Hibiscus syriacus
'Blue Bird'

Ceanothus x delieanus
'Gloire de Versailles'

Choisya ternata
'Sundance'

Perovskia
'Blue Spire'

Fuchsia magellanica
'Aurea'

Ceratostigma
wilmottianum

Santolina rosmarinifolia
'Lemon Fizz'

Caryopteris
clandonensis
Hint of
Gold'

Yucca gloriosa 'Bright Star' underplanted with Hedera helix 'Green Ripple'

Late Summer Border

The planting scheme in the plan shown is aimed at a peak display in late summer. The many blue-flowered species flowering at this time of the year suggest a colour theme to which yellows and orange are added. The *Malus* 'Golden Hornet' will give golden crab apples and the *Pyracantha*, orange berries. Winter colour and structure come from the variegated *Ilex*, *Choisya* and *Pittosporum*, and the *Yucca* specimens will give strongly architectural shapes. Although at its flowering peak in late summer, there is plenty of foliage interest throughout the seasons.

should revel in the dappled shade of a woodland. Low groundcover could be provided by *Gaultheria shallon* and *Cornus canadensis*.

For low maintenance, a mix of shrubs and groundcover plants can be very effective, providing due attention is given to a selection of species

This simple planting of **Hydrangea paniculata** provides a stunning contrast to the soaring architecture of this Paris church.

with contrasting textures and shapes and interest at various seasons. Good examples would be *Potentilla*, *Viburnum davidii* and *V. tinus*, *Skimmia japonica* 'Rubella', *Pyracantha* 'Orange Glow', *Prunus laurocerasus* 'Cherry Brandy', *Photinia* × *fraseri* 'Red Robin', *Mahonia japonica*, *Griselinia littoralis* 'Variegata', *Fatsia japonica*, *Euonymus fortunei* 'Blondy', *Cotinus coggygria* 'Atropurpurea' and almost any *Berberis*. Such plants will have a very low demand for maintenance and still give immense pleasure over many years. Avoid those such as a *Buddleja*, lavender, *Caryopteris*, *Santolina*, *Fuchsia*, *Cornus* and so on that need annual pruning.

More on plant associations

Shrubs and other woody plants including trees are important for providing the framework or skeleton of a garden because they, and the associations created between them, are effective at all times of the year. However, their effect can often be enhanced by the other plants that can be grown

with them. Herbaceous perennials, ornamental grasses, bulbs and to a certain extent annuals and bedding plants can all be used to associate with shrubs. The possibilities are limitless but, for example, you might have a plant of *Ceanothus* 'Blue Mound' next to the evergreen *Choisya* 'Sundance' for its rich golden foliage, and alongside a big clump of *Anchusa* 'Loddon Royalist' for its intense blue flower spikes. Each plant looks attractive in its own right, but together they make a pleasing composition.

Many bulbs associate well with shrubs, particularly those that tend to be more informal such as spring flowering *Narcissus*, *Crocus*, *Chionodoxa*, *Scilla* and *Muscari*. All these tend to establish easily, survive from year to year and build into bigger colonies. Hyacinths and tulips tend to look less effective with shrubs, probably being more at home in formal flowerbeds. They are also less successful in surviving from year to year without being dug up and stored. However, the species tulips and some of the smaller-flowered cultivars that bloom earlier in the year are more likely to be

With a colour scheme of gold and purple, plus varying heights and textures, this simple scheme has lots of interest.

successful when planted with shrubs. A successful spring border might include some *Skimmia japonica* 'Rubella' for its ruby buds, *Camellia* 'Donation' for its pink flowers and *Chaenomeles speciosa* 'Nivalis' for its white blossom. These could be underplanted with the spotty-leaved herbaceous *Brunnera macrophylla* 'Jack Frost', together with white *Narcissus* 'Thalia', the black-flowered *Fritillaria persica*, and *Anemone blanda* 'Radar' with vivid pink flowers.

For summer display you might try planting *Eucomis*, *Eremurus* or any of the members of the genus *Allium*, the ornamental onions. Try planting a group of *Sambucus* 'Black Lace' with *Rosa* 'Buff Beauty' for its soft apricot blooms and add the tall orange *Lilium lancifolium* 'Flore Pleno' in the front. The rose and elder together will give colour most of the summer, with a crescendo of colour when the lilies flower in late summer. Stunning!

SOURCING SHRUBS

It's relatively easy to make a list of the plants you want to grow but sourcing good specimens at an economic price can sometimes be a challenge.

Good gardens need good plants, so do take the trouble to find reliable suppliers. Don't buy cheap shrubs in plastic bags at a supermarket even if the coloured picture on the front looks attractive. They will often be dried out and are usually coarse, unimproved versions of common shrubs that will swamp a small garden. Avoid neighbour's giveaways unless you know exactly what you are being offered.

Where to buy

Your first stop should be one of the big warehouse DIY stores with a garden centre. Many have excellent plants at good prices, but don't expect experienced advice. These are sellers, not growers. Garden centres are similar and offer an amazing range of products and plants for the garden. Very few will grow their own plants but will usually have good quality and prices are likely to be reasonably competitive. Garden centre chains are likely to have newly introduced novelties as they are released. Some advice may be available.

Traditional retail nurseries where plants are grown on site and sold direct to the customer are far less frequent these days. Where they exist they can be an excellent source of good plants and

Plant fairs such as this are exciting events where you can purchase a huge range of unusual plants from the nurseries that produce them.

usually very good advice direct from the people who grow them. Prices will nevertheless reflect this and they are unlikely to be the source of a good bargain!

Many nurseries sell through specialist plant fairs that are run throughout the country, particularly in the spring, summer and autumn. These will often be located at a public garden or stately home at a weekend. Here you will find the cream of small nurseries, all offering the best they have at any one time. These are really good events at which to buy plants, particularly if you have become a bit discerning. Although prices may not be cheap, you have the opportunity to compare different sellers at close quarters all in one visit. Quite often several nurseries will have the same plants and you can check which are best or cheapest. Arrive early because unusual plants may be in short supply and it can be most frustrating to see just what you want in other people's bags!

Mail order can be very uncertain. Plants are likely to be either quite small or, if large, the carriage charges will be high. Mail order does have the risk of postal delay but suppliers will usually insure against plants being dead on arrival. Many specialist nurseries will have a website with an online ordering facility.

Many readers will have discovered eBay, the online computer auction, and this too has a gardening section. Often, some unusual plants can be offered and there is some assurance over supply because eBay sellers are rated and you can see if past customers have been pleased. Remember, though, that unless the seller happens to be local, whatever you buy has to come through the post.

Types of plant

Plants come in many different shapes and containers and a few terms are worth understanding before you order plants.

A 'bare root' or 'open ground' plant will have been grown in a field. These are dug up and the soil shaken from the roots. It is imperative that the roots never dry out and so bare root plants should always be wrapped. Such plants are often cheap but very vulnerable and unless they have been kept constantly moist may well be dying before you buy them. Bare root plants must be planted in the winter and it can be useful to soak the roots in a bucket of water for a short while before planting to ensure that they are moist.

A 'rootballed' plant is similar but has been dug with some soil and roots kept intact and wrapped in sacking or plastic. It is a technique often used for trees, conifers and evergreen shrubs such as rhododendrons. They are usually planted in winter but the season is a little less critical as there is less disturbance to the roots.

'Container grown' means that the plant has spent all its life in a pot of some sort. Container growing is used for many different types of plants and particularly for shrubs. Most shrubs are grown in 2 litre or 3 litre containers which are quite adequate for general planting and will establish

This healthy plant of *Berberis* 'Golden Torch' has a good bushy shape, is well clothed with foliage and its leaf colour is appropriate.

quickly. However, if you want an instant effect, or some impact from specimen plants, many suppliers will also offer 10 litre plants or bigger.

Selecting a good plant

All plants are different but a few basic principles will help you assess the value and health of a plant. Firstly, any plant should have good, healthy green leaves that do not show signs of pests or diseases. Remember, of course, that some plants are grown for their yellow or other coloured foliage. Any plant which has a tired, faded label, a dirty pot and moss all over the soil surface has probably been on display far too long and should be avoided.

It is often difficult to assess the roots of a plant but, if you can, gently knock the plant out. There should be a good proportion of strong young white roots showing. A pot full of old brown roots is an indication that the plant has been around rather too long. While looking at the roots, keep an eye open for vine weevils, which are small white grubs. They are serious pests that live on the roots of plants and can cause the total collapse of the plant. The biggest plants are not always the best. Look for plants that are stocky and sturdy and have a number of branches or side shoots. These will ultimately give the best garden display.

Good gardens are never finished

Really, there are no rules governing the composition of a good planting scheme. It all depends on innovation, an eye for good combinations, trial and error. The late Christopher Lloyd was once asked how he devised his wonderful planting schemes. He replied dismissively, and somewhat mischievously, that he put 'any old colours together'. Possibly he did put all colours together in an experimental way, wondering what the results would be, but it is likely he had some idea of the outcome. When he found successful combinations, he no doubt fine-tuned them and repeated them again in other parts of his garden.

Be prepared to tweak a planting scheme as it grows. Good gardens are never finished and there is always the opportunity to change things and improve on them, year by year. Take a critical eye to your garden and make notes during the summer when plants are in full growth so that changes can be made at the appropriate season.

A spectacular garden such as this looks mature but will need constant monitoring and occasional replants to keep it in peak condition.

7 GROWING SHRUBS

So far you have read the book, drawn a plan and maybe rushed out to fill a trolley with new plants. So now comes the hard work – get your gloves and boots on and find your spade, fork and barrow! Good soil cultivation is an absolute necessity for the success of any new planting scheme. Most shrubs are capable of growing and looking good for 10 to 15 years but this will depend on whether you can give them the ideal conditions to establish and all that they need in future years to promote healthy growth.

PREPARATION AND PLANTING

There is an old saying along the lines of 'Spend a penny on your plant and a pound on the hole'. Quite simply, don't get carried away with buying good plants without thorough preparation of the soil where you're going to grow them. Plants get almost everything they need from the soil, including water, nutrients and also air. Understanding your soil is an essential part of making sure your shrubs grow well. All soils are different and you need to learn about the soil in your own garden. In large gardens this may differ from one part to another.

Soils for shrubs

Firstly you need to assess the texture of the soil, which is a measurement of its basic components. In simple terms, if the soil feels gritty between

your fingers then it is likely to be a sandy soil. If you moisten some of the soil and rub it between your fingers, you will also be able to feel whether it is sticky, which indicates the presence of clay. A good mixed soil will have a balance of sand, silt and clay and is then usually called a loam. Sandy soils tend to be well drained and warm but dry out quickly in hot weather in the summer. Just right for Mediterranean plants such as lavender and *Cistus*. By contrast, clay soils are wet, heavy to cultivate but tend to stay moist in dry weather. Roses thrive in clay soils. Both types are improved by adding organic matter.

Also it's no good dreaming of a garden full of beautiful heathers, camellias and rhododendrons if your soil is chalky and alkaline. Quite simply, they won't grow! So you need to know whether your soil is acid or alkaline and this is measured on a scale called pH. Garden centres will have simple kits that you can use to assess the pH of the soil. A neutral soil, that is neither acid nor alkaline, will be around pH 7.0, which is a good level for growing many things. Plants such as rhododendrons will need an acid soil which will have a pH below 7.0. Chalky soils will have a high pH and in this situation you must carefully choose plants that are tolerant of chalk. Generally, sandy soils tend to have a low pH and be more on the acid side, suitable for rhododendrons, *Hamamelis* and camellias. Clay soils are likely to be somewhat more alkaline, with a high pH, and you could choose *Buddleja*, *Ceanothus*, *Escallonia*, *Viburnum* and many more. Always check the soil in a new garden or border before buying plants.

As well as these basic criteria for soils, there may be other factors that will affect a soil's value for growing shrubs and creating a garden. Bad drainage often occurs where the soil has been mistreated in some way. For example, the gardens of many new housing developments will have a thin skim of topsoil, often covering rubble and rubbish, under which is a layer of very heavily compressed soil that has been driven over by machines and vehicles during the construction period. Such a compacted and badly drained soil will be a very poor basis for a new garden. You must correct these issues by good cultivation and improved drainage if you want a great garden.

Good garden soils should also be rich with organic matter, which is often indicated by a darker colour and crumbly fibrous texture. Gardens linked to older houses that have been cultivated for many years often have poor, worked-out soils. In this situation it is essential to add lots of organic matter, such as compost or manure, to improve the soil and restore the soil's life.

Soil preparation

Cultivating your soil for planting is a straightforward and very satisfying gardening exercise but should be done thoroughly. If there are any perennial weeds such as couch, bindweed, docks or ground elder present, these must be eradicated before planting a new border. The simplest way of doing this is by using the translocated herbicide called glyphosate. This must be applied to the shoots of offending weeds and it then travels, destroying all parts of the plant including the root system. It is not effective during the winter months when weeds are dormant, so must be applied during the summer growing season. If you prefer not to use herbicides, then you can try slowly and methodically forking out all the roots of perennial weeds but it is a tedious job. Alternatively, cover the area with thick black polythene or an old carpet to smother the weeds. This will need to stay in place for at least six months to be effective, so it's a slow process. It is, however, essential to have a clean, weed-free site before planting new shrubs, as it will be exceedingly difficult to eradicate weeds after planting.

All borders should be deeply dug, breaking up any compacted soil. If possible do this in advance and leave it for several weeks so that the soil can settle and the weather can break down the surface. Incorporate plenty of good-quality organic matter such as compost or manure at the digging stage. Just before planting, apply a high phosphate fertilizer such as Enmag at 30g/m^2 (1oz/yd^2) or organic bonemeal at 60g/m^2 (2oz/yd^2) and lightly fork it into the soil surface. Any specialist soil changes for particular plants should be made at this stage. Don't be tempted to cut corners with hasty soil preparation.

Sometimes there may be a situation, such as a steep slope, where it is inappropriate to dig the entire area. Cultivating all the soil in such a situation would cause it to wash down to the bottom in heavy rain. Here it is better to prepare small pockets of loosened soil for each shrub, well enriched with organic matter and fertilizer. The surface can also be slightly dished after planting to help catch rain or irrigation water before it runs down the slope.

Planting shrubs

The traditional and ideal time for planting a new shrub border is winter. During this season the widest range of plants will be available and, once settled in, new shrubs will be able to slowly establish their roots over the cooler months before they need to make new leaves and shoots in the spring. During the winter months, some plants will also be available as open ground or rootballed plants. However, you can plant at any time of the year because most plants are available these days as container grown, but be prepared to water during dry weather if you plant in the summer months.

Always space out all your plants where you are intending to put them before starting any planting. This is particularly important if you have chosen not to make a plan in advance. If any plants are missing and due to arrive later, mark them with a cane or empty pot. Then stand back and look at the results before you actually dig the holes and plant the plants. Sometimes what you have planned doesn't look quite right when you go to plant it, but a little juggling between the plants and the spacing will usually give you a successful result.

This small town garden has made full use of a range of plants, including small trees, carefully spaced shrubs and herbaceous perennials, for a stunning effect.

Correct spacing is important to ensure that plants have adequate room to fully develop. A small magnolia plant with three or four twiggy branches will look nothing like the majestic 3m (10ft) specimen that it may well become in a few years. Most good shrub catalogues and books will give you an idea of the mature spread of a shrub as well as its height. This will enable you to space them and allow for ultimate growth. Remember that a shrub with a spread of 1.8m (6ft) next to one with a spread of 1.2m (4ft) will require an average distance between them, in this case 1.5m (5ft). Shrubs placed at the right density for their ultimate size will look quite sparse in their early years and it is quite acceptable to plant other, quick-growing plants such as herbaceous peren-

When planting a new shrub, dig a good-sized hole, knock the plant out carefully from its pot, position it in the soil and refill, firming the soil back around the roots.

nials, bulbs or bedding plants between them to fill the gaps. Alternatively, for quick effect many gardeners will plant shrubs in groups much closer than needed, with the aim of thinning at a later stage when the planting starts to thicken out.

Dig out a good-sized hole to accommodate the roots and if necessary break up the base of the hole with a fork. When you tip your plant out of its container, you may like to gently tease out any roots which have wrapped themselves tightly around the edge of the root ball. All shrubs, whether pot grown, open ground or rootballed, should be planted with the root systems only just below the new soil surface. Shovel back the soil, firm around the roots with your boots and rake the surface level.

Mulching

Finishing off with a good thick mulch of bark or other organic matter will help to keep new shrubs moist and speed up establishment. A good-quality, medium grade bark is probably the most attractive and effective mulch. Other materials are available such as spent hops, mushroom compost, leaf mould or garden compost. If you use the latter it is essential that it is thoroughly rotted in such a way that the weed seeds have been killed during the decomposition process. Also remember that spent mushroom compost has a high pH and should not be used with lime-hating plants like rhododendrons. You can also use inorganic materials such as gravel, pebbles or crushed slate. To be effective a mulch needs to totally cover the soil so that no weed seedlings can emerge. This means a depth of between 50–75cm (2–3in).

Establishing climbers

This may seem a very basic task, but there are a few tips which will help the success and quick establishment of a new plant. Climbers are often used against a wall, tucked amongst other plants, or to climb through an established tree. Whatever the situation, the new plant needs the best chance of growing away without undue competition. If you're planting against a wall, make sure that you

The owner of this garden has skilfully hidden a drainpipe behind a screen of canes being used to support a young clematis.

do not put the root ball closer than about 30cm (12in) from the wall. The soil adjacent to a wall is likely to be in a rain shadow and is usually very dry and impoverished, so plant away from the wall and lean the top of the plant in towards the trellis or support. The same principle applies when planting climbers to scramble through trees. If at all possible avoid planting right close to the trunk of the tree, where the soil will be highly compacted and full of roots. If possible plant a climber out at the edge of the tree canopy and lead the plant into the tree with a bamboo cane. You can often do this on the back of the tree so that it doesn't look too odd.

Do find out how a climber supports itself, so that you can give it the best possible opportunity to cover the space allotted. Climbers such as ivies and Virginia creeper will cling well to brick walls or rough surfaces once they attach themselves. Use a couple of bamboo canes to press the stems gently against the wall, so that as they grow they can easily latch on. Those climbers that have tendrils or twist their stems will need relatively thin supports around which they can easily twine themselves. The slender support of a trellis or obelisk will usually be quite enough for most climbers. But if you want such a climber to work its way up around the smooth poles of a pergola, you will have to either add some strings or wrap the pole with some plastic mesh. Initially it may help to spread out the stems and tie them into the support to encourage the climber to colonize the space allocated. Do avoid leaving climbers unattended for too long. A vigorous *Wisteria* will soon wrap several stems into a tight bundle that is difficult to disentangle and will not form a good basis for later flowering.

Climbing and rambling roses support themselves naturally by sending out long whippy stems which eventually drop under their own weight

PLANTING CLEMATIS

With clematis, you are advised to break the rules and plant the rootball deeper than normal, positioning it about 7.5cm (3in) below the soil surface. Clematis suffer from a wilt disease which can attack shoots above ground level. Should this occur, a deeply planted clematis stands more chance of surviving and regenerating from below the soil surface. Clematis like their 'heads in the sun and their feet in the shade', so mulch the roots well with any of the usual mulching materials or place some rocks or cobbles around the base. This keeps the root system cool and moist.

and then use their thorns to catch on the nearest object. This is unlikely to be suitable in most garden situations, so you will need to tie in the new stems to a support as they grow.

The climber *Passiflora caerulea* comes from South America but is hardy in the UK and flowers continuously through summer.

This particularly fine form of *Clematis montana* is sold as 'Tetrarose' and is just as easy to grow as the plain species.

You can get quite stunning effects by planting more than one climber in the same location. Clematis mix well with roses and honeysuckles. Obviously, for the full effect, both need to flower at the same time. Ivies mix well with deciduous climbers and their colourful evergreen foliage can be very welcome in the winter. Remember that you can also grow many climbers up established trees and shrubs. Old fruit trees are ideal for this technique. Try planting a *Clematis montana* 'Grandiflora', which will scramble through the tree almost unseen and then burst out all over the crown with masses of white flowers in late spring. You can also plant ivies at the base of old trees to cover the lower trunks. Cultivars such as 'Jester's Gold' will add an extra touch of winter colour to an otherwise drab corner. Vigorous shrubs like *Pittosporum, Rhamnus alaterna* 'Variegata' and *Corylus* are ideal homes for climber that

will scramble through the branches and pop out flowering shoots in unexpected places. Try planting the golden-leaved *Jasminum* 'Fiona Sunrise' to scramble through the ruby-red leaves of *Corylus maxima* 'Purpurea'.

AFTERCARE

Looking after a shrub border is not unduly onerous but do take particular care of it during the first couple of seasons when plants are young and establishing. Shrub plantings probably require less maintenance than any other type of display, so are ideal for low maintenance gardens. They need merely a few hours a week and will also tolerate being left for several weeks if you go away.

Maintaining new plantings

Maintaining a weed-free environment is good practice for establishing any plants and particularly so for a new shrub planting. If the soil surface has been mulched, there shouldn't be much weed growth but any weeds that do appear should be removed by hand or with the use of a hoe, taking care not to disturb the young roots of your shrubs. Any perennial weeds that appear can be dealt with by a very careful application of glyphosate, making sure that this does not contact any plants you want to keep. It's a good, safe weedkiller if used responsibly but will kill anything green it touches.

During dry spells, you must water to ensure that your young shrubs are not stressed. This should be done using a hose and a sprinkler to thoroughly soak the entire area, only repeating when it has completely dried out once more. Just damping over the surface is not effective.

Pruning should not be necessary during the first couple of seasons with most new shrub plantings. It is generally best to leave shrubs to grow naturally on their own. However, any unduly vigorous shoots that seem to grow out of proportion to the rest of the plant can be shortened back to encourage a bushy habit. Also look out for any plants such as rhododendrons or maples

A mature shrub border such as this will have a low maintenance requirement, but will need annual pruning, feeding and mulching.

that may have been grafted. Any growths from the rootstock will appear as strong shoots from near ground level and if these have emerged from beneath the union, which should be quite clear, they should be removed completely. Shrub roses will sometimes produce suckers from beneath the ground and these should be removed by grasping firmly using a thick glove and pulling away from their point of origin.

Seasonal maintenance

Each spring is a good time to review shrub plantings and carry out some basic maintenance. To keep shrubs healthy and growing well, apply a general fertilizer such as Growmore or an organic feed such as blood, fish and bone, both at $60g/m^2$ ($2oz/yd^2$). For flowering shrubs you could ideally use a fertilizer with more potash, and for foliage and stem growth one with high nitrogen, but a general balanced fertilizer is usually effective for mixed plantings. Top up the mulch if it's looking sparse. If you can see soil through a mulch, then it's too thin and won't be doing its job.

At this time of the year, buy replacements for any gaps that have developed. Treat gaps as opportunities to try new plants and give a fresh look to your borders. After a hard winter you may have shrubs damaged by the cold. Scrape the bark on the stems carefully with a fingernail or knife.

If it's green and moist underneath, the plant is still alive and likely to regrow. If it's brown and hard then the stems are dead. Sample lower down the plant to find out whether it is all dead. If the lower parts of the plant are still alive, prune out the dead parts. Some shrubs will regenerate from their roots even if all the top growth is dead.

Traditionally, gardeners often fork or even dig over the surface of borders, particularly during the winter months. Although this may provide a tidy appearance, it actually serves no valid purpose. Such disturbance is bound to sever surface roots, bury your mulch and have a negative effect on your plants. Such cultivation will also bring weed seeds to the surface and actually increase the weed problem. Don't waste your effort on this.

Shrubs tend to be fairly free from pests and diseases and in general it is best to leave them alone and avoid spraying. However, because of their age and size young plants are likely to be more easily affected by pests and diseases, so if these do appear you may wish to try and control them. Details of various problems are dealt with later in this chapter.

Moving a large woody plant

Sometimes a large shrub, such as a magnolia, may outgrow its space but is too good to just throw away. In this situation it is quite possible to move

Mixed borders contain herbaceous perennials as well as shrubs and so will need more complex maintenance, but the effect is probably worth the extra effort.

it, if some advance preparations are made. Ideally you will organize this a year in advance by digging around the base at least 20cm (9in) away from the stem to sever any major roots. Refill the trench you have created with some good soil or old potting compost and this will encourage new fibrous roots that will be easy to transplant.

A year later, during the winter, the plant will be ready to move. You can prune back the top growth by up to a third if you wish as this will reduce the shock to the plant. Dig around the plant again, slightly further out from last year's trench and you should find a band of strong new fibrous roots which must be carefully protected. Go all the way round the plant and then dig carefully under it, trying not to damage the root ball. When the whole structure is loose it needs to be physically moved to its new location; it may be useful to wrap the roots with polythene if it is likely to be out of the ground for more than a few minutes. Big rootballs can also be very

heavy so handle carefully, possibly sliding it on a board.

Reposition the plant in its new location and refill with good soil, staking carefully with a diagonal stake to avoid breaking up the rootball. Water thoroughly and mulch with a deep organic mulch. If the plant is an evergreen, spray it over with an anti-transpirant that can be obtained from most garden centres, which primarily stock it to prevent needle drop in Christmas trees. This will slow the rate of water loss from the leaves and encourage establishment.

Growing shrubs in containers

Many shrubs will grow successfully in large pots for a number of years. Probably those that are most effective will be evergreens and those described as architectural plants with an interesting shape. For example, *Cordylines* make excellent container specimens, as do *Yuccas*. Evergreens such as box, bay, holly or yew trimmed into ornamental shapes have a very simple classic effect. They are often available as pre-trimmed cones, pyramids and standards or you can grow your own. When bay trees are grown as standards, they are sometimes grown with curly stems. Other useful species include *Pittosporum, Choisya, Elaeagnus, Fatsia japonica, Camellia* and a whole host of different bamboos, all of which make excellent container specimens.

Use a container that is in proportion to the size of the shrub you are displaying but that will also allow for a fair amount of additional potting compost, to allow the roots of the shrub to grow and develop. Ideally, move plants on to a larger container each year. If this doesn't make sense, then try and scrape away some of the old compost each spring and replace with new. One style of traditional container, originally used for growing citrus trees, is known as a Versailles Caisse. These are wooden containers with four removable sides, so that each year one side can be opened to enable some of the old compost and roots to be removed and replaced with new. When growing shrubs in containers, it is best to use a loam-based potting compost such as John Innes Potting Compost No 3. Adding a slow release fertilizer at the potting stage and every twelve months in spring will also ensure healthy nutrition for containerized shrubs. Don't forget to water regularly in the summer months.

Growing shrubs in containers can also be useful as a temporary home for those plants that most gardeners buy on impulse, often not having a permanent home for them at the time of purchase. Pot them on, maybe in just simple terracotta pots, and display them as a small ornamental group. By the time you have decided on a permanent home for them, they will probably have doubled in size.

PESTS AND DISEASES

Fortunately, shrubs in general do not suffer from a great number of pests and diseases and it is only occasionally that you are likely to have to treat them for any problem. Keeping plants well fed,

This azalea is being grown as a bonsai in a shallow container and will require specialist attention and regular watering.

The best defence against pests and diseases is to grow shrubs well, with adequate food and water to give a robust constitution.

watered when dry, and growing in well-drained soil results in healthy growth that will have greater resistance to pests and diseases. Mixed plantings are also likely to attract a range of beneficial creatures that will control pests naturally. There are, however, a few problems that may occur and will need controlling. Whenever possible it is best to use a biological control or a safe organic pesticide. Occasionally it may be necessary to use a more potent pesticide and on those occasions great care should be taken to follow the instructions and safety recommendations.

Pests

Shrubs are likely to host a wide variety of insects and spiders, many of which will be entirely harmless or beneficial and so generally live in a happy equilibrium, causing little or no damage. Just a few are serious pests and may cause major damage that needs attention.

Cushion scale

Evergreen shrubs such as camellia, holly, rhododendron and *Euonymus japonica* are attacked by this sap-sucking pest. Although long established in the UK, it has become more widespread and troublesome over the last twenty years. It excretes honeydew, causing infested plants to develop a thick, black, disfiguring coating of sooty mould over the winter months. Yellowish-brown, oval scale insects up to 3mm (⅛in) long can be seen near the veins on the undersides of the leaves. Rectangular, white, waxy egg masses, up to 1cm (½in) long and 2-3mm (⅛in) wide, are produced by the adult scales in early summer and the remains of these egg masses persist on the foliage throughout the year.

On a small area, scale insects and their eggs can be removed by wiping the foliage with a damp cloth. For a major infestation, spray with a systemic pesticide containing thiacloprid, thiamethoxam or acetamiprid. Contact sprays containing deltamethrin will also give control if applied thoroughly to the underside of leaves. Organic pesticides, based on plant oils or extracts, may be effective but will need to be applied repeatedly to clear the pest.

Rabbits

This may seem a strange inclusion under pests and diseases, but these creatures can absolutely decimate young shrub plantings to the point of death. Rabbits seem to have an amazing appetite and to be able to devour very tough foliage, including plants with prickly leaves and thorns! Whenever planting a new border in a rural location, or even a town situation, it is wise to check whether there are rabbits in the area.

Protecting new plantings from rabbits is a major exercise, requiring the use of fine mesh wire netting which must be sunk in the ground at least 20cm (9in) deep to prevent rabbits tunnelling under. In some situations it may be worth protecting the whole garden and eradicating rabbits from the enclosed area. There is a commercial product that achieves some success by making plants unpalatable to rabbits but application needs to be repeated about every six weeks. The material is safe, containing calcium and trace elements that break down into products that plants can use.

Some plants seem less attractive to rabbits and it may be worth trying a selection of these when

Rhus typhina 'Laciniata', from North America, makes a large bush and is likely to be resistant to rabbit attack.

RABBIT-RESISTANT PLANTS

Arundinaria	Fatsia japonica
Aucuba japonica	Hydrangea
Buddleja davidii	Ligustrum
Berberis	Philadelphus
Buxus	Prunus laurocerasus
Ceanothus	Rhus
Choisya ternata	Rosmarinus officinalis
Cistus	Sambucus
Cornus alba	Skimmia japonica
Cytisus	Syringa vulgaris
Daphne mezereum	Viburnum tinus and opulus
Elaeagnus	Yucca

planting shrubs in problem areas. However, what is palatable to rabbits seems very variable from area to area and in a cold winter, when food is scarce, rabbits will eat an amazing range of plants including prickly species such as roses, berberis and mahonia.

Viburnum beetle

The larvae of this pest cause the most damage, eating holes in the leaves of many species of viburnum in the spring and leaving them badly damaged and discoloured. The larvae are about 9mm (½in) long, creamy yellow with black markings, and are likely to be present from late spring through to early summer. Chemical control is possible where large numbers are present, using deltamethrin, thiacloprid or pyrethrum.

These small grubs are the larva stage of the viburnum beetle and their voracious feeding badly damages young foliage.

Vine weevil

This pest has become noticeably more prevalent in recent years and can be found on a wide range of plants, particularly those in greenhouses and nurseries, so it can sometimes be unwittingly imported with new plants from a garden centre. The adult vine weevil is an ugly greyish beetle with long antennae that eats notches out of leaves. It disfigures plants but rarely causes major damage. The larva, which is the young stage, is a small white grub up to 1cm (½in) long with a brown head. This stage causes major damage because the grubs live on the roots of plants, causing wilting and, if unchecked, death. Established plants in the garden can usually withstand an attack but young plants in pots, with small root systems, will be badly affected.

If vine weevil is suspected in a potted plant, the simplest treatment is to tip it out and examine the roots. If infected, wash the roots thoroughly, removing the infected compost and grubs. Repot in fresh compost and keep in a damp atmosphere until re-established. Surprisingly, plants will often recover such drastic treatment. With a more widespread problem, it is possible to use a chemical root drench containing acetamiprid. Alternatively, a biological product based on a nematode (*Steinernema kraussei*) is available from suppliers of biological controls; this parasitizes the weevil. On mild spring or summer evenings inspect plants and walls by torchlight and pick off the adult weevils. Shake shrubs over an upturned umbrella to dislodge and collect the weevils. Trap adults with sticky barriers such as Agralan Insect Barrier Glue placed around pots or on greenhouse staging. Vine weevils and their grubs are eaten by a variety of predators such as birds, frogs, toads, shrews, hedgehogs and predatory ground beetles.

Aphids

All sorts of greenfly and blackfly may attack various shrubs in the garden. Although they may occasionally be disfiguring, they will rarely cause major damage. In most gardens, natural predators such as ladybirds will provide sufficient control.

Diseases

There are relatively few diseases that affect shrubs but those that do are nearly all fairly destructive, so if observed they should be dealt with promptly and thoroughly before they spread.

Armillaria

A wide range of trees and shrubs are attacked by this disease. It is also known as honey fungus because of the groups of honey-coloured toadstools that are eventually produced. Initially it will show as a general yellowness of leaves, followed by wilting. Quite quickly the plant will start to die and large trees can go from apparent health to death within a single season. It quickly spreads from plant to plant through the soil; so, for example, on privet, which is particularly susceptible, you can see the disease working its way down a hedge.

The presence of this disease can be confirmed in two ways. Scrape the bark near ground level and check for the presence of a white mould that smells of mushrooms. Alternatively, dig down to the root system and look to see if there are any black, thread-like growths. These give the disease the name 'bootlace fungus' that is sometimes used.

The control of armillaria is very difficult. Initially, infected plants should be dug up and burnt. There is a soil drench containing cresylic acid that can be used to prevent further spread and this is worth using if there are other valuable trees or shrubs nearby. Soil infected with armillaria can only be used for some years for non-woody plants such as annuals, herbaceous plants and vegetables. Replacement of the soil is possible but large quantities will usually have to be dug out and it is difficult to be sure that all the fungus has been removed.

There is a small risk of importing armillaria with woodchip or bark mulch. The risk is low with proper commercial mulches that have been composted at high temperatures. The risk is

These honey coloured toadstools are a symptom of an advanced stage of the disease *Armillaria* which will have infected woody plants and surrounding soil.

Amongst the healthy foliage on this *Pyracantha* there is evidence of die-back, likely to be caused by fireblight, that must be cut out.

greatest with uncomposted wood chippings direct from an arborist, which may have been produced from infected trees.

Box blight

This is a disease that has become prevalent in recent years. Initially it causes small spots on the leaves that spread to produce dead patches and defoliation. The disease is harboured by dead leaves that remain on the ground, so good hygiene and tidiness underneath box hedges is essential. There are no real control measures, although encouraging strong growth helps the plant to become resistant. Also avoid trimming box hedges in warm, damp weather as the fungus is inclined to enter through open wounds.

Coral spot

Red pustules appearing on dead twigs are the first sign of this fungal disease. It sometimes spreads into living tissues, and the golden-leaved *Elaeagnus pungens* 'Maculata' seems particularly prone to infection. Generally make sure dead wood is thoroughly pruned out of shrubs and when coral spot is observed, make sure you prune well back beyond the obvious infection. Infected wood must be burnt.

Fireblight

Members of the rose family, such as pyracantha and cotoneaster, are likely to be affected by this disease. Flowers, leaves and twigs turn brown, shrivel and eventually blacken. It looks as if they have been burnt. It can easily be spread by rain splashes, birds, insects or on gardening tools. As soon as infected shoots are observed, they should be pruned out well beyond the damaged areas and the infected material burnt. Sterilize pruning tools with bleach or alcohol.

The yellow areas between the veins, correctly called interveinal chlorosis, signifies a lack of iron caused by a high soil pH.

Hypericum rust

Fortunately this fungal disease only affects hypericums, causing orange spots on the undersides of the leaves, which eventually drop. The common Rose of Sharon, *Hypericum calycinum*, can be affected and the cultivar 'Elstead' is particularly susceptible. There is no easy cure but pruning hard to the ground and removing and burning all debris is likely to reduce the risk of a recurrence the next year, when the plants regrow.

Phytophthora ramorum

This disease began to cause the widespread death of oak trees in the USA in the 1990s and is sometimes called sudden oak death. It also affects *Rhododendron*, *Viburnum*, *Camellia* and *Pieris*, whilst a related disease also attacks *Magnolia* and *Ilex*. It was not identified in the UK until 2002. It is primarily a disease that threatens nursery stock but there have been outbreaks in garden situations. It causes brown lesions on leaves, leading to larger spots of dying tissue, leaf drop and then die-back of shoots. Infected plants must be burnt and as this is notifiable disease, any outbreaks must be reported to the local Plant Health Inspector, who will be part of Department for Environment, Food and Rural Affairs (DEFRA).

Lime-induced chlorosis

A deficiency of iron is very common on alkaline soils and shows as yellowing between the leaf veins (interveinal chlorosis). It readily shows with plants such as *Rhododendrons*, *Camellia* and *Pieris* growing on chalky soils. This is not actually a disease as such but a nutritional problem. It is corrected by watering with sequestered iron, which is readily available in garden centres.

8 SHRUB PRUNING

'If they block windows or paths, prune them, otherwise leave them alone' is basic but very good advice. Pruning is probably one of the least understood jobs in the garden. So often shrubs are badly pruned both by amateurs and, sadly, even more often by professional gardeners who should know better. Commercial landscapers and local authorities often prune shrubs with hedge trimmers into shapeless, flowerless blobs and the result is ugly to say the least! In general, if there is no particular reason for pruning or you do not know the correct technique, then shrubs are better left alone.

REGULAR PRUNING

Having said that, there are some shrubs that will give better displays with regular pruning, and there are a few simple techniques that are easily understood. With all types of plants you can remove any dead, weak, diseased or dying shoots to maintain the health of the shrub. Also remove any branches that are crossing or too closely spaced to look attractive. All pruning cuts should be made just above a bud. Beyond that, it all depends on how the plant grows, when it flowers, or if the display is from foliage or coloured stems. Understanding a few basic rules will enable you to prune the majority of familiar shrubs correctly. Once mastered, pruning is a very satisfying job!

Do buy a good pair of secateurs with a comfortable grip. The best ones are called bypass secateurs and behave rather like a pair of scissors with two

OPPOSITE: **An essential tool for all shrub pruning is a good pair of sharp secateurs, used here to remove a reverted shoot.**

blades that slide alongside each other. Anvil secateurs are likely to be cheaper and have one blade that closes against a flat surface. If not sharp they tend to crush the stems you are pruning. And remember that like all cutting tools, secateurs will need sharpening from time to time. In addition, a small pruning saw is useful for large branches, or alternatively a pair of loppers, which are like tough secateurs with long handles. A small garden shredder can be useful for dealing with prunings; after shredding they can be composted and will make an ideal mulch to go back on your borders.

Very few shrubs need formative pruning while they are young, although you may shorten the occasional vigorous shoots that grow out of proportion to the others. A few plants such as *Cornus controversa* 'Variegata' have a habit like a small tree and with these it is advisable to encourage one main shoot, usually called the leader, and shorten any competitors.

In general, with healthy mature shrubs, the harder you prune the stronger the regrowth, so hard pruning to restrict size is rarely successful. It is better to reduce the length of just some of the stronger shoots and repeat this later. The result is likely to be a gradual reduction of the size of the shrub without ruining its shape or destroying its flowering potential.

Flowering shrubs

The season of flowering is all important: prune at the wrong time of the year and you will lose all the flowering potential. Many fast-growing shrubs such as *Buddleja* (butterfly bush), *Ceratostigma*, *Perovskia*, *Caryopteris*, *Ceanothus* 'Gloire de Versailles', *Hydrangea paniculata* and hardy fuchsias all flower in late summer. As such, they have the whole of the summer to grow and produce flower buds and so can be pruned in the spring each year. These are hard pruned back to a short permanent framework. Vigorous growth will follow, which then matures and flowers the same season.

The line drawings in this chapter show the different types of pruning. Red marks show where the pruning cuts are made; the shoots that remain are coloured; and those that are removed are outlined in black and white.

With spring and early summer flowering shrubs such as *Forsythia*, remove a proportion of the older flowered branches.

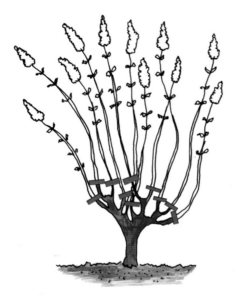

Late summer flowering shrubs like *Buddleja* are hard pruned to a short framework, removing all old growth.

Forsythia, Weigela, Ribes (flowering currant), *Philadelphus* (mock orange), *Kerria japonica, Deutzia* and *Jasminum nudiflorum* flower in late spring or early summer and are also fairly fast growing. They should be pruned immediately after flowering to allow them to make fresh growth, ripen their wood and initiate flower buds before autumn and winter dormancy. The pruning technique here is not so harsh and this group should only be thinned, removing the oldest flowered shoots and leaving young shoots to mature for next year. It is usually easy to tell the oldest wood because it will be twiggy, often darker, and have the remains of the flowers hanging on it. New shoots, which will usually be single, whippy and often green in colour, must be left. As these mature over the summer, side shoots will develop and next year's flower buds form. These will remain dormant through the winter and then burst into life to flower the next spring or early summer.

Cytisus also flower in early summer and are one of the few plants that can be legitimately trimmed with shears, as they have multiple stems. Do this immediately after flowering. However, be sure not to cut back into the old wood because *Cytisus* will not regrow. Only trim into the previous year's green shoots.

Coloured-stem and foliage shrubs

The dogwoods, members of the genus *Cornus*, various white-stemmed *Rubus* and coloured-stemmed willows such as *Salix daphnoides*, 'Britzensis' and 'Dart's Snake', need hard pruning in mid spring to encourage vigorous regrowth, which will be your brightly coloured display for the next winter. Pruning is right down to almost ground level and is sometimes called 'stooling'. Ideally, this is done every winter and followed with a dressing of general fertilizer to stimulate new growth. Alternatively you can do it every two years, or even thin the plants, removing 50 per cent of the growths each year. If you don't prune regularly they soon become huge tangled bushes full of old wood that becomes dull.

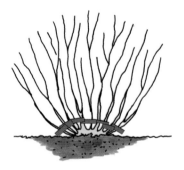

Dogwoods and willows grown for their colourful stems are stooled, which involves pruning all stems hard to ground level.

Many foliage shrubs also respond well to hard pruning. *Santolina* in all its forms and *Artemisia* 'Powis Castle' both get very straggly without pruning and the flowers on both are insignificant. Prune hard each spring. Also other foliage plants such as *Cotinus coggygria* 'Atropurpurea' and 'Golden Spirit', coloured-leaved *Sambucus*, *Spiraea* 'Goldflame', *Weigela florida* 'Variegata' and *Eucalyptus* all respond well to cutting back hard. This results in strong lush growth on a compact bush and large, intensely coloured leaves.

Renovating overgrown shrubs and hedges

Sometimes shrubs grow so big that they totally outgrow the space allocated to them and become problems. Trimming and regular pruning rarely solve the problem, often spoil the shape and display of the plant and need to be repeated frequently. In such a situation it is well worth cutting hard back to a stump 15–20cm (6–9in) high. This can be done at any time but late winter

VARIEGATION AND REVERSION

Occasionally, variegated shrubs will send out shoots that are plain green rather than variegated. Such shoots will tend to grow much faster than the rest of the plant as they contain a larger proportion of chlorophyll within the leaves. If they are not removed, there is the risk that they will take over and that the more attractive coloured-leaved parts of the plant will tend to die back. Always remove any plain green shoots back beyond the reverted tissues.

Plain green shoots appearing on variegated shrubs such as this *Griselinia* are known as reversions and should be pruned out.

A mature yew hedge undergoing renovation, showing height reduction and pruning on one side.

Then feed, mulch and water during the following summer and the hedge should regrow strongly. The next spring you can repeat the procedure on the second side. Trim the new growth regularly to get a nice tight green barrier. Mid spring is the best time to renovate hedges.

Shrub roses

Shrub roses generally require very little pruning and can be left alone for the first few years. After a while they become congested, the general vigour and flowering may decline and they will start to show dead wood. Prune them by removing a few old branches, up to one third, as low as possible in the bush. You can also lightly tip back weak shoots and remove the remains of last year's flowers and hips. Time this for midwinter, when the leaves have dropped and the plant's structure is easy to examine. This pruning will encourage new growth from the base and fresh vigour. Ideally repeat this process each year.

Climbers

Most climbers and wall shrubs require discreet pruning to keep them within the area allocated

is probably the best time. Follow this with a good balanced spring feed and a mulch. Such a plant will regrow back into a natural shape and soon resume its flowering pattern. With a few shrubs such as rhododendrons, which are likely to have been grafted, you must be careful that such pruning does not go below the graft line or only the rootstock will regrow. Relatively few shrubs are grafted, so this is not a common issue.

Hedges have the bad habit of getting bigger each year until you suddenly find that they are far taller than intended and greedily swamping your valuable garden space. Provided a hedge is healthy, you can rejuvenate it and reduce it considerably in size. Most familiar species will respond well, including yew and box, but conifers will not respond. The process takes two years. In the spring of the first year, reduce the hedge down to just below the height that you want and cut back on one side hard to the main framework, which will become apparent as you start to prune.

Shrub roses should have a few old branches removed completely to ground level and any weak shoots and shoots with remaining rose hips should be tipped back.

and also to ensure that they do not extrude too far from their support. Most climbers have their own mechanisms for attaching themselves but wall shrubs will usually need to be tied back to the trellis or wires used to train them. During this process some of the more wayward branches will need to be removed. This should be no more than a thinning process, to ensure that flowering wood is not removed. This is very much a generalization. Many plants such as *Pyracantha*, *Fremontodendron*, *Ceanothus* and *Abutilon* do not actually require pruning to encourage flowers, so the less we remove the better.

Clematis are the exception and the pruning required will depend on the species or cultivar and the time of year of flowering. They are generally divided into three groups for pruning purposes.

To a certain extent, you can vary the severity of the pruning. With Group 2 clematis, a harder prune will tend to encourage more late summer flowers and fewer early blooms. With Group 3 cultivars, you can alter the height of the display by where you make your pruning cuts. So if, for example, you want a 'Perle d'Azur' to scramble over an apple tree, you might only prune it to

1.8m (6ft) from the ground, which will give it extra stature and allow the blooming growths to extend further.

The ornamental vines such as *Vitis coignetiae* and *V. vinifera* 'Purpurea' should be hard pruned in early winter before the sap has started to rise for spring growth. In the initial years after planting you should allow the strong growth to extend until it has covered the area allocated. From then onwards annual pruning will involve cutting back all lateral shoots to two or three buds from the main framework.

Wisteria needs regular pruning to keep the size under control and also to stimulate flowering growth rather than just leaves. When young, you can allow a wisteria to grow fast to encourage it to fill its allotted space. Once established, it should be pruned twice a year, in late summer and then again in late winter. In late summer, after flowering, cut back all the whippy green side shoots of the current year's growth to five or six leaves. This controls the size of the wisteria, preventing it getting into guttering and windows, and encourages it to form flower buds rather than just leafy growth. Then in late winter cut back the same

CLEMATIS PRUNING GUIDE

	Pruning	Examples
Clematis Group 1 Early flowering clematis, generally small-flowered and flowering on old wood.	Only prune when they exceed their allotted space; this should be done immediately after flowering, so that the new shoots have time to grow and mature.	C. montana C. alpina C. macropetala C. armandii and all their hybrids
Clematis Group 2 Early to mid-season flowering, large-flowered clematis, flowering early on old wood and also later on new wood.	Prune in early spring by trimming back shoots to the point of strong growth and plump buds. Remove any dead or weak shoots.	'Henryi' 'Lasurstern' 'Nelly Moser' 'Niobe' 'The President'
Clematis Group 3 Late summer flowering, large-flowered cultivars, blooming on current year's wood.	Prune in early spring, cutting all the stems back to about 20cm (9in) from ground level, which will result in vigorous regrowth.	'Ernest Markham' 'Etoile Violette' 'Huldine' 'Ascotiensis' 'Ville de Lyon'

growths to two or three buds. These short stubby side shoots will become the flowering wood, very much like spur pruning apples.

Don't prune

Slow growing shrubs such as *Rhododendron*, *Camellia*, *Viburnum*, *Daphne*, *Ilex* (holly), *Syringa*, *Hamamelis* (witch hazel), *Mahonia*, *Chimonanthus* and *Skimmia* do not need regular pruning. The occasional leggy or wayward shoot can be reduced but otherwise do not prune.

Lilacs can have the dead flowerheads removed for the sake of tidiness and to conserve the plant's energies. Do this by cutting back just to the next pair of buds after flowering. Rhododendrons also benefit from a similar treatment, although this can normally be done by pulling the dead flowerheads off with the fingers. The dying flowerheads of mophead hydrangeas actually look quite attractive in their brown skeleton form and, as most are

An established *Hydrangea* bush in spring being pruned to remove last year's dead flower heads just above the new flower buds.

sterile, there is no seed production. Leaving them on over the winter also protects next year's flower buds. In spring prune back lightly, removing the old flowering stem back to the prominent, fat

WISTERIA STANDARDS

Although *Wisteria* is a climber, it makes an excellent small standard specimen and can look spectacular when in full bloom with a cascading waterfall of blue blossoms.

Start with a young, single-stemmed plant and tie it to a stout cane or stake, 1.2–1.5m (4–5ft) tall. If growing in a pot, John Innes No 3 potting compost is essential because a mature plant can be top heavy. Twine the stem around the support in the right direction. *Wisteria sinensis* has stems that twine anticlockwise, but *Wisteria floribunda* twines clockwise. Allow the main shoot, the leader, to grow unchecked until it reaches the top of the support and then remove the tip the following winter to encourage the formation of side shoots at the top of the stem. Prune the side shoots the following winter, shortening them to 15–30cm (6–12in) and repeat this process each winter to gradually build up a head. As the head develops, prune in late summer as well. Each winter, cut back the side shoots to 2.5cm (1in) of their bases, just as you would routinely prune a wall-trained plant. Remove any shoots that appear from the main stem.

Wisteria is a fast-growing climber, so it will not take many years to make an impressive display like this old specimen.

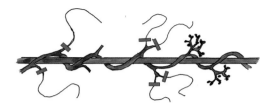

Part of a *Wisteria* stem showing the successive stages of summer and winter spur pruning to encourage flower buds.

Removing the old flowerheads from rhododendrons to prevent seed pod formation will encourage the flower buds forming for the next year.

buds beneath, which will be the coming summer's flowers.

Do not prune spiky foliage plants such as *Cordyline* or *Yucca*. If necessary, remove dead leaves but otherwise leave untouched. Avoid pruning conifers and never cut back hard into the old wood as they will not regrow. Old canes on bamboos can be thinned out but otherwise do not prune.

SHUB PRUNING AT A GLANCE

Type of Shrub	How to Prune	Season	Examples
Late summer flowering shrubs	Hard prune all growths	Early spring	*Buddleja, Caryopteris, Ceratostigma, Perovskia, Hydrangea paniculata*
Spring and early summer flowering shrubs	Thin out, removing old flowered wood	Immediately after flowering	*Forsythia, Deutzia, Philadelphus, Kerria, Jasminum nudiflorum*
Coloured-stem shrubs	Hard prune to ground (stooling)	Early spring	*Cornus, Salix, Rubus*
Foliage shrubs	Hard prune to ground (stooling)	Early spring	*Santolina, Artemisia, Cotinus, Sambucus*
Shrub roses	Thin, removing up to third of old branches	Winter	All shrub roses
Slow-growing shrubs	No pruning		*Camellias, Daphne, Ilex, Hamamelis*
Vines and wisteria	Spur prune back to framework	Winter	*Vitis coignetiae, Wisteria*
Spiky plants	Removal of flowered shoots only	Any time	*Yucca, Cordyline*
Bamboos	Thin, removing old canes remove side shoots	Any time	*Phyllostachys, Fargesia, Himanobambusa*
Conifers	No pruning or minimal trimming	Spring	*Juniperus, Chamaecyparis*

9 PROPAGATING SHRUBS

Many shrubs are relatively easy to propagate and it can be exciting and profitable to grow your own. Seeing cuttings root and grow on into usable plants and eventually mature shrubs can be very rewarding. A supply of new plants is always useful in a garden, enabling you to replace plants that have died, fill gaps or landscape new areas. A nicely grown shrub is also a very welcome gift and a nice change from a bottle of wine when you go to visit friends. Some enterprising gardeners have also made small but useful extra ventures, growing their own shrubs and selling at car boot sales or on eBay. If you decide to do this, do make a good job of it, using good pots, proper potting composts and feeding your new shrubs adequately. If you follow a few basic guidelines there is no reason why you cannot produce shrubs every bit as good as those produced by commercial nurseries and at minimal cost.

Although it may take two years to produce a shrub ready for planting, the only real costs are the pot and the compost to fill it. Beyond that it is just your own skill and patience. So it's almost all profit!

Do remember that some plants are protected by Plant Breeders' Rights, which are like a patent or copyright. Nurseries wishing to propagate them commercially must obtain a licence and pay a fee for each plant propagated and sold. Individuals may propagate them for their own use and to give away but it is illegal to propagate and sell without paying the fees. The labels of protected plants will usually include information about this.

OPPOSITE: With virtually all propagation by cuttings, it is important to choose non-flowered shoots or to remove any flower buds.

PROPAGATION FACILITIES

Shrubs can be propagated by rooting cuttings, by layering, from seed or by grafting and budding. Rooting cuttings is probably the most widespread. Ideally, you will have a greenhouse for propagating shrubs, although a polythene tunnel can be equally successful. Rooting cuttings requires a humid atmosphere and warmth and these are best supplied with the use of an electric propagator. These are relatively simple, thermostatically controlled units that will keep your cuttings warm and humid. They are not expensive and make a good investment if you propagate plants each year. If you don't have a greenhouse or polythene tunnel, site the propagator on a windowsill indoors. Small mist propagation units are available for amateur greenhouses and these do provide almost ideal conditions for rooting cuttings, so may be worth considering if you root a lot of them.

Cleanliness is essential for plant propagation. Young seedlings or rooting cuttings are very vulnerable and can easily fall prey to a number of damping-off or rotting diseases. Although it may be possible to control these, it is better to avoid them and this is done by good hygiene. Always use clean pots and fresh compost. Never be tempted to use rainwater out of a water butt or storage tank for seedlings or propagation, as it will very likely be contaminated with various fungal infections. Make sure that greenhouses are kept tidy and that the areas under the benches do not become repositories for rubbish, and homes for pests and diseases.

Composts

Plant propagation requires various different potting composts – these are the growing media that you will need for propagation and growing plants in containers, and are not to be confused with compost produced from rotting down garden waste. Seed composts have very low nutrient levels and are used for seed sowing. Potting composts will have more nutrients and are used for pricking out seedlings and potting young plants. Proprietary mixes are likely to be more reliable than a home-made mix. A propagation compost for rooting cuttings can easily be made by mixing sand and peat, or peat and fine bark, in equal proportions. There are also many multipurpose composts available, which do not perform ideally for any one function but will be adequate for most purposes and avoid the need for lots of different bags. They have low nutritional levels, so additional liquid feeding must start at an early stage.

Most modern composts are loamless, which means they are without loam (soil). Many are based on peat, although there is a move away from all peat composts for environmental reasons. Non-peat or reduced peat composts are available, based on materials such as coir, bark, wood chips or other recycled materials. Although these can produce acceptable results they are nowhere near as easy to use and the results can be disappointing. Peat-based composts generally remain the most predictable and effective.

You can also still obtain a traditional range of growing media called the John Innes Composts and these are very good for some uses. Being based on loam, they tend to be heavy, which is a disadvantage when carrying the plants but can be an advantage in a windy area as plants do not blow over so easily. They tend to produce good sturdy plants but growth is often slower than in loamless composts. There is a John Innes Seed Compost, then three potting composts with increasing levels of nutrition, which for short are often labelled JIP1, JIP2 and JIP3.

SHRUB CUTTINGS

Many shrubs can be easily propagated by taking cuttings. This is a simple technique that generally involves the removal of a piece of a plant, which is then induced to produce its own roots and become established as an independent plant. The trick with all cuttings is to encourage them to produce roots without the cutting drying out or dying before it is able to survive on its new root system. This is what propagation is all about!

Sharp knives, secateurs, suitable rooting composts and a selection of pots and trays are the

A small plastic propagator like this is suitable for rooting cuttings from all manner of shrubs in summer and early autumn.

basic requirements. Hormone rooting powders can also be very useful and speed up the process of rooting, particularly with difficult subjects. These are synthetic products but are based on natural auxins that exist in all plants. Although it is not essential to use rooting powder with all cuttings, it is particularly advantageous with plants that are difficult to root or when conditions are not ideal, such as early or late in the season. Most cuttings will prefer to be rooted in a heated propagator within a greenhouse but successful results can be achieved with a cold frame or on a windowsill.

Tip cuttings

The simplest type of cutting is a tip cutting, which is used for propagating many shrubs at different times of the year but particularly in summer and autumn. This is prepared by removing the tip of a shoot and reducing it to about 75mm (3in) with about three leaves. The actual number of leaves will depend on their size; for example, you might leave two pairs of leaves on a cutting of *Weigela* and perhaps six leaves on a cutting of *Potentilla* as the leaves are much smaller. With some plants such as *Hydrangea*, which have very large leaves, you can actually reduce the size of the leaves by cutting them in half with a sharp knife. The base of the cutting is trimmed just below a joint which is correctly known as a node. The lower leaves should be removed to leave a bare stem

Such a cutting can be dipped into hormone rooting powder and then inserted into a pot of rooting compost. Several cuttings can usually be inserted around the edge of a pot. A 9cm (3.5in) pot will usually hold three cuttings nicely, and a full-size seed tray, 35–48 cuttings. Do not mix different cuttings in the same tray or pot as they may well take different times to root.

ABOVE LEFT: **Trimming a *Euonymus* cutting just below a leaf joint.**

ABOVE CENTRE: **Removing excess lower leaves with a sharp knife.**

ABOVE RIGHT: **Dipping the prepared cutting in hormone rooting powder.**

BOTTOM LEFT: **Inserting a group of cuttings in a pot of rooting compost.**

ABOVE LEFT: **Conifer cutting being trimmed with lower leaves already removed.**
ABOVE CENTRE: **Wounding a conifer cutting to expose the cambium for rooting.**
ABOVE RIGHT: **A pot of conifer cuttings, labelled and ready for the propagator.**

Firm in gently and water thoroughly. Do make sure you label cuttings carefully, particularly if you are propagating similar plants. Cuttings have no roots and so we must ensure that they remain as moist as possible. This is done by either placing them in a closed propagating frame or within a plastic bag.

Softwood cuttings are usually prepared in late spring or early summer when growth is lush, and this technique is used particularly for propagating deciduous shrubs such as *Potentilla*, *Hypericum*, *Philadelphus* and *Forsythia*. Later in the season, growth will start to harden and feel rubbery and is then suitable to use for semi-ripe tip cuttings. This is the best season for taking cuttings of evergreen shrubs and conifers. For example, plants such as *Hebe*, *Euonymus*, *Griselinia* and *Escallonia*, as well as junipers and *Thuja*, will root well at this time. Conifers are slow to root and can be encouraged by removing a sliver of bark at the base of the stem before dipping in rooting powder. This is called wounding and exposes more of the cambium tissues, which are the part of the stem that produces new roots. Hollies are also slow to root and will benefit from being wounded and treated with hormone rooting powder before insertion. Sadly there are no longer any fungicides available to amateurs for controlling botrytis, which causes cuttings to rot off. Therefore be very careful to use clean trays, new compost and clean water. If any cuttings show signs of damping off during rooting, remove them immediately to avoid spread.

CUTTINGS WITH SILVER FOLIAGE

Shrubs such as *Lavandula*, *Santolina*, *Artemisia*, *Helichrysum*, *Phlomis* and *Brachyglottis* (formerly *Senecio*) all have soft velvety silver foliage and do not respond well to conditions during rooting that are too humid. They are most successful when propagated by semi-ripe cuttings in early autumn. Instead of placing them in a closed propagating frame, try laying a sheet of very thin clear or white polythene loosely over the trays or pots of cuttings. This will give some humidity without the wet conditions that could rot the cuttings. Each day remove the sheet of polythene, shake it lightly and replace it with the dry side down. Such a technique is usually successful for most silver foliage cuttings.

Silver-leaved shrubs like this are best rooted under a light polythene covering rather than in a humid propagator.

Leaf bud cuttings

A few plants produce stems that are not conducive to preparing as ordinary tip cuttings. For example, clematis makes very long whippy stems with widely spaced leaves. With clematis you can cut up the stems, positioning each cut just above a leaf joint. Discard the very soft tip and then shorten each of the cuttings to about 7.5cm (3in). These leaf bud cuttings are then inserted until the node touches the compost, which will be the point from which both the roots and the new shoot are produced. You can also propagate all the various types of *Hedera* by this technique.

The tip of a *Mahonia* shoot is large and bulky and would be very difficult to make into a single cutting. Again, cut up the shoot into pieces, each of which will consist of a small 2cm (1in) section of stem, a node, a leaf and a dormant bud. The compound leaves are quite long so reduce the size by trimming them back to about three pairs of leaflets.

Propagating heathers

All members of the genera *Erica, Calluna* and *Daboecia* are easily propagated. If you need large quantities of plants, you can prepare tiny softwood tip cuttings in midsummer, each cutting being about 2cm (1in) long. Although easy to root, these will take at least a couple of seasons to produce a usable plant. Alternatively, in early autumn prepare larger cuttings consisting of older shoots with several side shoots. These branched cuttings need to be about 5cm (2in) in overall length. When rooted, you will already have small multi-stemmed plants that will grow into a usable size within a year. Remember to use an acid potting compost for growing many heathers.

Finally, you can try mound layering, which is the easiest of all. Quite simply take some rooting compost and work a few handfuls down into the crown of an existing heather plant, all around the base of the shoots. You can do this at almost any season but make sure the plant and new compost are kept moist. About three to six months later check the plant and you should then be able to gently pull apart and sever shoots that have rooted into the new compost.

These branched heather cuttings will root over winter and be ready for potting up in early spring.

IMPROVISED PROPAGATION

Many common shrubs can be easily propagated on a shady windowsill with simple equipment. A plastic bag can be used to cover a pot of cuttings, with the base secured with an elastic band. The bag should be removed on a daily basis and turned inside out so that the cuttings do not stay excessively wet. Alternatively, the base of a plastic soft drinks bottle can be removed and used as a tiny propagator to cover a small pot of cuttings. Again it should be wiped out each day to avoid a build-up of excess moisture. Cuttings of many plants can easily be rooted in two to three weeks in this way.

You can also try propagating with very simple conditions and minimal protection. Prepare a small bed in a shady area of your garden, incorporating extra sand and peat or compost into the surface to give a good rooting zone. Do this in late summer for use with semi-ripe cuttings and try both evergreens and deciduous shrubs. Cuttings are prepared in the normal way and inserted in rows direct in the soil. Water in thoroughly, ideally using a liquid fungicide. Cover the area of cuttings with a small polythene tunnel, such as you would use for protecting salads or seedlings in the vegetable garden. You can also improvise with a small wooden box without a base, either covered with a sheet of glass or with polythene tacked over the top. The covering should only be removed if watering is necessary, otherwise leave the unit untouched until well into the following spring, by which time your cuttings should have been rooted. You can then remove the cover and allow them to grow on where they are for the rest of the summer, lifting them the following autumn either to plant out or to pot up and grow on. This is a very simple and economical way of rooting some easy common shrubs.

Hardwood cuttings

These are prepared from leafless stems in winter and the technique is used for easy deciduous shrubs such *Buddleja, Forsythia, Salix, Symphoricarpus, Physocarpus, Hypericum, Weigela* and shrub roses. They can be prepared from about late autumn to midwinter by cutting up stems into sections about 20cm (9in) long. These should be trimmed just above a bud at the top and just below a bud at the bottom. As they have no leaves they do not require fussy conditions for rooting so can be inserted in a trench in the garden. Lining this with sand improves drainage and helps to

Trim hardwood cuttings below a node at the base and above a node at the top.

Insert hardwood cutting into pots of rooting compost or in a trench outdoors.

avoid the cuttings rotting if the winter is wet. They should be inserted deeply about 15cm (6in) apart, leaving no more than two or three buds above ground. Be sure to insert them the right way up and gently firm the soil round them. They will not root and grow away until next spring but growth is often fast and young plants will be ready for transplanting the following autumn. Hardwood cuttings can also be rooted in deep pots in a cold greenhouse but do not try to speed them up with heat.

GROWING ON SHRUBS

Most softwood and semi-ripe cuttings will take between two to six weeks to root, although some will be slower. Tug gently to see if new roots have formed and replace the cutting if it comes straight

out. Once rooted, they need to be weaned. A rooted cutting is a new plant capable of life on its own, but it is still fragile. You should slowly acclimatize rooted cuttings to normal conditions, removing them from the propagator but still keeping them lightly shaded and damped over for a few days.

After weaning, rooted cuttings should be potted up into 9cm (3.5in) pots using potting compost. Place them in a cold frame or unheated greenhouse, watering as necessary. Keep them shaded and damped over until settled in their new pots. Softwood cuttings will probably be ready for potting up midsummer after rooting. Semi-ripe cuttings, if rooted quickly, can be potted up in late autumn, but if rooting is slow the cuttings should be left in their rooting trays and not potted up till the following spring. Although these cuttings and small plants are from hardy shrubs, it is advis-

ABOVE LEFT: **A nicely rooted *Euonymus* cutting, ready for potting.**

ABOVE CENTRE: **Potting into a 9cm (3.5in) pot, using potting compost.**

ABOVE RIGHT: **Cover the roots with compost and firm in gently.**

LEFT: **Water in carefully and grow on in a cold greenhouse.**

able to give them some protection during the first winter while they are young and vulnerable. A cold greenhouse, polythene tunnel or cold frame is quite adequate and over the winter months you should try to keep this well ventilated when weather conditions allow.

Different shrubs will grow at varying rates, so you will have to be aware of their progress in order to time various tasks. The nutrition in most potting composts is exhausted within about four to six weeks, so after that time you will need to start feeding with a balanced, all-purpose liquid feed. Feeding would normally continue through-out the spring, summer and autumn months but stop during the winter. As growth develops, it is useful to pinch out the top of your young shrubs to encourage bushy growth. Do this when they are about 7.5cm (3in) tall. At this stage they are sometimes called 'liners', because in a traditional nursery they would have been ready for lining out in a field. Most shrubs, if growing well, should be ready to move on to larger pots some time during the year following rooting.

For most shrubs this will be the final potting, so you should use either 2 or 3 litre pots. Most shrubs will make a quite acceptable plant in a 2 litre container, but anything fast-growing such as buddleja can go into the larger 3 litre pot. Any plants that are growing very slowly, such as conifers, should be potted into 1 litre pots as an interim measure. When roots grow too slowly and the compost is not properly colonized, there

RECYCLED POTS

Many nurseries, garden centres and landscape contractors nearly always have surplus plastic pots available. Most commercial organizations do not reuse them, although they will often send them away for recycling. As there is usually a cost for this process, they are often quite happy to give away plastic pots that they do not want. Such pots have usually only been used once and will often be in very good condition. Always ask before raiding any waste area, but the owners will often be quite happy for you to take away waste pots. There is a very small risk that they might be harbouring disease organisms but it is minimal. Clean them thoroughly before reusing and they should be fine. If you sort them when you collect them, you can get a fine batch of smart-looking pots that will enhance the plants you are producing.

is the risk that it will remain wet and become sour. Again, use a good-quality potting compost. Young shrubs, even quite small plants, can be prone to blowing over in windy conditions so it is useful at this stage to use the potting compost that contains some grit or sand to give extra stability. It

Knocking out a young *Euonymus* plant twelve months later.

Potting on to a 2 litre pot, again using potting compost.

The full sequence from unrooted cutting, through rooting, growing on, first-year 'liner' to finished plant ready for planting after two years.

is also well worthwhile adding some slow-release fertilizer to the compost and mixing it well in before potting.

Your new shrubs will take probably another year to grow into usable or saleable plants. This is very much a generalization as it depends on the species and speed of growth, but for most common shrubs it is a two-year process between taking cuttings and having a finished plant. During this final year they can stand outside, ideally in a sheltered spot with gravel underneath to provide good drainage. Make sure they are well watered throughout the season. Any weeds appearing in the surface of the compost should be removed. As growth continues you can lightly

Pyracantha berries being 'sown' and covered with grit prior to standing outside for stratification by winter frosts.

trim any leggy shoots to encourage a bushy habit. You must also be aware of any pests or diseases and take appropriate measures.

OTHER PROPAGATION METHODS

While many shrubs can be rooted from cuttings and this is often the preferable way for a commercial nursery or in the back garden, there are other techniques that are sometimes used. Seed, layering and grafting are all slow methods, and grafting requires a high level of skill.

Growing from seed

Shrubs can be grown from seed but remember that hybrids will not breed true, so it is generally only useful for species plants. You can try *Cotoneaster horizontalis*, *C. microphylla* and *C. lacteus*, *Berberis wilsonea* and *B. julianae*, *Cytisus scoparius*, *Ilex aquifolium*, *Pyracantha rogersiana*, *Mahonia aquifolium* and *Paeonia delavayii* var *ludlowii*, all of which are easy to germinate. If you collect from hybrid cultivars, the results may be anything, but who knows – you might be lucky enough to find the next best-selling novelty!

Many shrub seeds will not germinate immediately because they have a dormancy factor. This means that the seed needs particular conditions to trigger it into growth. Seeds of many hardy plants such as holly or cotoneaster need a period of cold or actual freezing before they will germinate. This means that seed must be sown in the autumn and left outside, exposed to the cold over winter. This is sometimes called stratification. Such seed will then often germinate freely in the spring.

Shrub seeds are usually sown in deep pots and covered with a layer of fine grit. With species such as *Cotoneaster*, where the seed is in a small berry, you can sow the whole fruit as this will break down over time. Protect the seeds with a layer of fine chicken netting to keep out mice and birds and leave the containers in the shade of a north wall. Check the pots at regular intervals to ensure that they do not become dry. Nothing much will happen over winter but by mid spring small seedlings should have appeared. These can be pricked out and grown on like other young shrubs.

Other seeds, such as members of the genus *Cytisus* and *Genista*, have very hard seed coats and would naturally be very slow to germinate. We can speed this up by scarifying the seed. This means that in some way we gently break through the hard seed coat to allow water to penetrate and germination to start. Some seeds can be nicked with a knife; others will need a small file, sandpaper or a hacksaw to penetrate through the hard seed coat. Following this with a soaking in water is also often beneficial for many such seeds. Most seeds of hardy shrubs are quite tough and will germinate outside without the need for a greenhouse or any fussy conditions.

Shrub seedlings can be pricked out into small pots and grown on like any other young shrubs as described above. Although they do not need any protection or heat, you may find it easier to look after small seedlings in a cold greenhouse.

Layering

This is rather like taking a cutting but without severing the shoot from the parent plant, so it is much easier to carry out. It is useful for many hardy shrubs, especially those that are otherwise difficult to propagate. Magnolias, wisteria and clematis can be rooted in this way. A suitable flexible young shoot is bent down to the ground. At the point where it will touch the ground, a small incision is made in the stem to partially sever it. Hormone rooting powder can be dusted over the cut. The shoot is then pegged down and the cut area gently buried, ideally in a suitable rooting

LEFT: **A low-growing shoot of *Vitis coignetiae* pegged down into a pot of compost for rooting as a layer.**

CENTRE: **A branch of a *Magnolia* being wrapped with polythene containing rooting compost as an aerial layer.**

RIGHT: **This grafted shrub shows the union, the join between the rootstock and the scion that will become the top growth of the plant.**

compost that must then be kept moist. Layers may take several months to root, according to the time of year they are started. When rooted, the stem connecting the layer to the parent plant is first severed. A few weeks later the plant can be lifted and transplanted or potted for growing on.

With some plants there may not be a suitable shoot near to ground level, so we have to perform the layering procedure higher up the plant; this is called aerial layering. Sphagnum moss was traditionally used for this procedure but is becoming increasingly difficult to obtain, so a multi-purpose compost can be used. Once again the stem is nicked, the wound treated with rooting powder and packed with either moss or compost to stop it closing. A polythene sleeve is then constructed around the stem and packed with the rooting media. Make sure it is moist and then seal the polythene securely above and below the rooting site. Rooting is often slow and may take many months. When roots start to show against the polythene, the aerial layer can be severed from the parent plant and potted up on its own or planted out into a new location.

Grafting and budding

These are complex methods of propagation that are generally used by professional nurseries to produce trees or rare shrubs. It is a highly skilled process and usually beyond the resources of most amateur gardeners. As well as acquiring the neces-

SHRUB PROPAGATION AT A GLANCE

Type of Plant	Method	Season	Examples
Deciduous shrubs	Softwood tip cuttings	Early summer	*Deutzia, Potentilla, Hypericum, Spiraea*
Deciduous shrubs	Hardwood Cuttings	Winter	*Weigela, Cornus, Salix, Buddleja*
Evergreen Shrubs	Semi-ripe tip cuttings	Autumn	*Hebe, Pyracantha, Escallonia*
Climbers	Leaf-bud cuttings	Summer/autumn	*Clematis, Hedera, Jasminum officinale*
Climbers	Layering – easy method	Summer	*Vitis, Wisteria, Clematis*
Difficult shrubs	Aerial layering – easy method	Spring	*Magnolia, Mahonia, Rhododendron*
Difficult shrubs	Grafting – often under glass	Spring	*Rhododendron, Acer, Syringa*
Conifers	Semi-ripe tip cuttings, wounded	Autumn	*Juniperus, Thuya, Chamaecyparis*
Shrub roses	Hardwood cuttings	Winter	*R. rugosa, R. glauca, R. moyesii*
Heathers	Semi-ripe branched cuttings	Autumn	*Erica, Calluna, Daboecia*
Silver-leaved shrubs	Semi-ripe cuttings	Autumn	*Artemisia, Lavandula, Santolina*
Species shrubs	Seed – stratified	Winter	*Ilex aquifolium, Cotoneaster lacteus*
Species shrubs	Seed – scarified	As soon as ripe	*Cytisus scoparius, Genista hispanica*

sary skills, grafting requires a source of the correct rootstocks for whatever species needs grafting. Grafting and budding are really only used when no other propagating technique works effectively. When a single bud is used, it is called budding, whereas a shoot that is attached is called a graft. Budding is the traditional technique used for propagating roses.

The rootstock will often be the basic wild form of a fancy tree or it may be a specially produced rootstock. Either way it will always be closely related. So, for example, the fancy dwarf maples such as 'Bloodgood' and 'Senkaki' will be grafted on the plain *Acer palmatum*, and fancy rhododendrons will be grafted onto a strong growing type such as 'Cunningham's White' or *R. ponticum*. Sometimes, when the modern Inkarho rootstock is used, the scion is grafted onto a short shoot of the rootstock and the whole composite structure rooted as a cutting. The same conditions that stimulate rooting are conducive to encouraging the graft union to form. The end result will be a fusion consisting of the rootstock of one plant joined to the top growth of another. In later life, with even quite mature trees and shrubs, you can often see the join, which is called the union.

Micropropagation

This is a modern method of rapid commercial propagation used to produce large numbers of plants by means of tissue culture. All plants are identical, generally disease-free and have a high viability and growth rate. In the past it might have taken many years to produce commercial stocks of a new plant, which would then be highly expensive. Using micropropagation, saleable stock can be ready in a much shorter span of time. However, the investment is high and the techniques are based on laboratory facilities and growth rooms, rather than traditional nursery techniques. While generally impractical for the amateur gardener, it is nevertheless a fascinating technique that has brought us many wonderful new shrubs.

Wonderful new plants such as this *Hydrangea* 'Teller Rotschwanz' can be rapidly bulked up for distribution using modern micropropagation techniques.

FURTHER INFORMATION

WHERE TO BUY SHRUBS

Retail nurseries

Bluebell Arboretum and Nursery
A specialist nursery growing a huge range of unusual trees and shrubs. Small arboretum with many unusual species. Mail order and visitors. Bluebell Nursery, Annwell Lane, Smisby, near Ashby de la Zouch, Derbyshire, LE65 2TA.
www.bluebellnursery.com

Crûg Farm
A specialist nursery with many unusual plants, some from their own plant hunting expeditions. Mail order and visitors. Crûg Farm Plants, Griffith's Crossing, Caernarfon, Gwynedd, LL55 1TU.
www.crug-farm.co.uk

Hilliers Nursery and Garden Centres
A large organization, supplying many garden centres throughout the UK. Also online mail order.
www.hillier.co.uk

Notcutts
Another large chain of garden centres supplied from a linked nursery. Mail order supplying the UK.
www.notcutts.co.uk

Pan-Global Plants
A specialist nursery with many unusual plants, some from their own plant hunting expeditions. Pan-Global Plants, The Walled Garden, Frampton Court, Frampton-on-Severn, GL2 7EX.
www.panglobalplants.com

The Place for Plants
A vast list of unusual and popular plants, garden, arboretum and plant centre. Mail order. The Place for Plants, East Bergholt Place, Suffolk, CO7 6UP.
www.placeforplants.co.uk

Wholesale nurseries

Bransford Webbs Plant Company
Many new introductions, suppliers to garden centres.
www.bransfordwebbs.co.uk

Fitzgerald Nurseries
Commercial propagators and producers of nursery stock.
www.fitzgerald-nurseries.com

Garden Beauty
Wholesale nursery specializing in *Hebe* and other shrubs.
www.gardenbeauty.co.uk

Genesis
Marketing organization responsible for promoting many new plant introductions.
www.genesis-plantmarketing.co.uk

John Woods Nurseries
Commercial propagators and wholesale nursery based in Suffolk.
www.johnwoodsnurseries.co.uk

New Place Nurseries
Propagators and producers of plants for the garden centre market.
www.npnurseries.com

WHERE TO SEE SHRUBS

Botanic gardens
Kew, Oxford, Cambridge, Ness, Edinburgh and many others, often linked with universities and having primarily a research and academic basis. Many botanic gardens will only grow plants of wild origin and so cultivars will not be grown.
www.britainsfinest.co.uk/gardens

Capel Manor Gardens
Thirty acres of beautiful gardens which include the trial gardens linked with the magazine *Which? Gardening*.
www.capelmanorgardens.co.uk/tag/which-gardening-trial-gardens

Four Seasons Garden
Award winning private garden near Birmingham, full of shrubs, bamboos, conifers and many other plants. It is open to visitors under the National Gardens Scheme in early summer.
www.fourseasonsgarden.co.uk

Sir Harold Hillier Gardens
Formerly the Hillier Arboretum; 180 acres of beautiful landscape filled with an amazing 42,000 plants from around the world.
www.hants.gov.uk/hilliergardens

RHS Gardens
Wisley, Hyde Hall, Rosemoor and Harlow Carr Gardens. Four beautiful and extensive gardens owned and managed by the Royal Horticultural Society and all open to the public. Plants well labelled. Trials of a whole range of plants including shrubs. Each has an extensive garden centre stocking a wide range of plants.
www.rhs.org.uk/Gardens

Savill Gardens and Valley Gardens
Both in Windsor Great Park; extensive plantings of rhododendrons and ericaceous plants in both gardens. Savill Gardens also has a wide general plant collection including a New Zealand Garden and a new rose garden.
www.theroyallandscape.co.uk/

USEFUL SHRUB INFORMATION

Websites

http://mygarden.rhs.org.uk/blogs/
RHS new plants blog by Graham Rice: a chatty blog that gives regular and detailed information on new plants, with good illustrations.

www.bredbypetermoore.co.uk
Bred by Peter Moore, an independent plant breeder responsible for a number of recent introductions.

www.nccpg.com
Plant Heritage, formerly the National Council for the Conservation of Plants and Gardens. Leading plant conservation organization, responsible for co-ordinating National Collections.

www.rhs.org.uk/rhsplantfinder
Royal Horticultural Society Plant Finder: an online database listing suppliers of more than 70,000 plants available from over 600 nurseries. Also available in book form. Definitive source for correct plant names.

www.rhs.org.uk/Media/PDFs/Advice/Pesticides
'Pesticides for Amateur Gardeners' is an excellent guide produced by the Royal Horticultural Society that lists currently available products and their uses.

Suppliers

Grazers
Rabbit control: a useful product for deterring rabbits. Grazers Ltd, Gill Bank Farm, Ousby, Penrith, Cumbria CA10 1QA.
www.grazers.co.uk

Nemasys
Suppliers of simple environmentally friendly pest controls. Becker Underwood Ltd, Harwood Industrial Estate, Harwood Road, Littlehampton, BN17 7AU.
www.nemasysinfo.co.uk

BOOKS ON SHRUBS

Notcutts Book of Plants
A very useful small book, derived originally from the Notcutts catalogue; first produced in 1961 but now in its seventeenth edition. Short pithy descriptions of a huge range of plants, plus an invaluable blue pages section, with over fifty lists of 'Plants for a Purpose'.

The Hillier Manual of Trees and Shrubs
A classic reference book first published in 1972, reprinted and updated, now listing over 10,500 woody plants. Includes conifers, bamboos and climbing plants. Detailed text but very few pictures. A good thorough reference manual.

RHS A-Z Encyclopaedia of Garden Plants
A very weighty tome that covers the whole range of garden plants, including shrubs. Highly authoritative and well-illustrated with high quality photographs.

INDEX